Love Not the World

Watchman Nee

Love Not the World

TYNDALE HOUSE PUBLISHERS, INC.
Wheaton, Illinois
CHRISTIAN LITERATURE CRUSADE
Fort Washington, Pennsylvania

Library of Congress Catalog Card Number 77-083585
ISBN 0-8423-3850-0, paper
Copyright © Angus I. Kinnear.
First published in 1968.
American edition published in 1978
by Tyndale House Publishers, Inc.,
Wheaton, Illinois 60187,
by permission of Kingsway Publications, Ltd.,
Eastbourne, Sussex, England.
Printed in the United States of America

98 97 96 95 94

22 21 20 19 18

Contents

Preface

The greater part of this book derives from a series
of addresses on the subject of "the world" given
by Mr. Watchman Nee (Nee To-sheng) of Foo-
chow to Christian believers in Shanghai city in
the early period of the Sino-Japanese War. They
are thus colored a little by the economic pressures of those days. To them have been added
other talks on the same general theme given at
various places and times during the period
1938-41. For example, Chapter Three is based on
a sermon preached at a baptismal service in May

1939. I am indebted to several friends for the notes which have supplied the book's source material.

The author sees the *kosmos* as a spiritual entity behind the things seen, a force always to be reckoned with. He deals with its impact upon the Christian and his impact upon it, with the conflicting claims upon him of separation and involvement, and with the destiny of the man in Christ to "have dominion." As always, Mr. Nee's studies display original thinking and he is not afraid to be provocative, stirring both heart and mind to a response. It is my prayer that, despite the inevitably piecemeal construction of the book, its theme will prove to have coherence as a picture of the man of God in the world, and further, that it may challenge us all who name the name of Christ to move more courageously and positively through this earthly scene, with thought always for our role here in God's eternal purpose concerning his beloved Son.

ANGUS I. KINNEAR

London
1968

1
The Mind Behind the System

"Now is the judgment of this world: now shall the prince of this world be cast out. And I, if I be lifted up from the earth, will draw all men unto myself" (John 12:31, 32).

Our Lord Jesus utters these words at a key point in his ministry. He has entered Jerusalem thronged by enthusiastic crowds; but almost at once he has spoken in veiled terms of laying down his life, and to this heaven itself has given public approval. Now he comes out with this great twofold statement. What, we ask ourselves, can it have conveyed to those who have just acclaimed him, going out to meet him and accompanying him home on his ride? To most of them his words, if they had any meaning at all, must have signified a complete reversal of their hopes. Indeed the more discerning came to see in them a forecasting of the actual circumstances of his death as a criminal (verse 33).

Yet if his utterance destroyed one set of illusions, it offered in place of them a wonderful hope, solid and secure. For it announced a far more radical exchange of dominion than even Jewish patriots looked for. "And I ..."—the expression contrasts sharply with what precedes it, even as the One it identifies stands in contrast with his antagonist, the prince of this world. Through the Cross, through the obedience to death of him who is God's seed of wheat, this world's rule of compulsion and fear is to end with the fall of its proud ruler. And with his springing up once more to life there will come into being in its place a new reign of righteousness and one that is marked by a free allegiance of men to him. With cords of love their hearts will be drawn away from a world under judgment to Jesus the Son of man, who though lifted up to die, is *by that very act* lifted up to reign.

"The earth" is the scene of this crisis and its tremendous outcome, and "this world" is, we may say, its point of collision. That point we shall make the theme of our study, and we will begin by looking at the New Testament ideas associated with the important Greek word *kosmos*. In the English versions this word is, with a single exception shortly to be noticed, invariably translated "the world." (The other Greek word, *aion*, also so translated, embodies the idea of time and should more aptly be rendered "the age.")

It is worth sparing time for a look at a New Testament Greek Lexicon such as Grimm's. This will show how wide is the range of meaning that *kosmos* has in Scripture. But first of all we glance back to its origins in classical Greek where we find it originally implied two things: first *a harmonious order or arrangement,* and secondly *embellishment or adornment.* This latter idea appears in the New Testament verb *kosmeo,* used with the meaning "to adorn," as of the temple with goodly stones or of a bride for her husband (Luke 21:5; Rev. 21:2). In 1 Peter 3:3, the exception just alluded to, *kosmos* is itself translated "adorning" in keeping with this same verb *kosmeo* in verse 5.

(1) When we turn from the classics to the New Testament writers we find that their uses of *kosmos* fall into three main groups. It is used first with the sense of the *material universe, the round world, this earth.* For example, Acts 17:14, "the God that made the world and all things therein"; Matt. 13:35 (and elsewhere), "the foundation of the world"; John 1:10, "he was in the world, and the world was made by him"; Mark 16:15, "Go ye into all the world."

(2) The second usage of *kosmos* is twofold. It is used (a) for *the inhabitants of the world* in such phrases as John 1:10, "the world knew him not"; 3:16, "God so loved the world"; 12:19, "the

world is gone after him"; 17:21, "that the world may believe." (b) An extension of this usage leads to the idea of *the whole race of men alienated from God and thus hostile to the cause of Christ.* For instance, Heb. 11:38, "Of whom the world was not worthy"; John 14:17, "whom the world cannot receive"; 14:27, "not as the world giveth, give I unto you"; 15:18, "If the world hateth you ..."

(3) In the third place we find *kosmos* is used in Scripture for *worldly affairs: the whole circle of worldly goods, endowments, riches, advantages, pleasures, which though hollow and fleeting, stir our desire and seduce us from God, so that they are obstacles to the cause of Christ.* Examples are: 1 John 2:15, "the things that are in the world"; 3:17, "the world's goods"; Matt. 16:26, "if he shall gain the whole world, and forfeit his life"; 1 Cor. 7:31, "those that use the world, as not abusing it." This usage of *kosmos* applies not only to material but also to abstract things which have spiritual and moral (or immoral) values. E.g., 1 Cor. 2:12, "the spirit of the world"; 3:19, "the wisdom of this world"; 7:31, "the fashion of this world"; Titus 2:12, "worldly (adj. *kosmikos*) lusts"; 2 Pet. 1:4, "the corruption that is in the world"; 2:20, "the defilements of the world"; 1 John 2:16, 17, "all that is in the world, the lust ... the vainglory ... passeth away." The Christian is "to keep himself unspotted from the world" (James 1:27).

The Bible student will soon discover that, as the above paragraph suggests, *kosmos* is a favorite word of the apostle John, and it is he, in the main, who helps us forward now to a further conclusion.

While it is true that these three definitions of "the world," as (1) the material earth or universe, (2) the people on the earth, and (3) the things of the earth, each contribute something to the whole picture, it will already be apparent that behind them all is something more. The classical idea of *orderly arrangement or organization* helps us to grasp what this is. Behind all that is tangible we meet something intangible, we meet a planned system; and in this system there is a harmonious functioning, a perfect order.

Concerning this system there are two things to be emphasized. First, since the day when Adam opened the door for evil to enter God's creation, *the world order has shown itself to be hostile to God.* The world "knew not God" (1 Cor. 1:21), "hated" Christ (John 15:18) and "cannot receive" the Spirit of truth (14:17). "Its works are evil" (John 7:7) and "the friendship of the world is enmity with God" (James 4:4). Hence Jesus says, "My kingdom is not of this world" (John 18:36). He has "overcome the world" (16:33) and "the victory that hath overcome the world" is "our faith" in him (1 John 5:4). For, as the verse of John 12 that heads this study affirms, the world is under judgment. God's attitude to it is uncompromising.

This is because, secondly, as the same verse makes clear, *there is a mind behind the system.* John writes repeatedly of "the prince of this world" (12:31; 14:30; 16:11). In his Epistle he describes him as "he that is in the world" (1 John

4:4) and matches against him the Spirit of truth who indwells believers. "The whole world," John says, "lieth in the evil one" (5:19). He is the rebellious *kosmokrator*, world ruler—a word which, however, appears only once, used in the plural of his lieutenants, the "world rulers of this darkness" (Eph. 6:12).

There is, then, an ordered system, "the world," which is governed from behind the scenes by a ruler, Satan. When in John 12:31 Jesus states that the sentence of judgment has been passed upon this world he does not mean that the material world or its inhabitants are judged. For them judgment is yet to come. What is there judged is that institution, that harmonious world order of which Satan himself is the originator and head. And ultimately, as Jesus' words make clear, it is he, "the prince of the world," who has been judged (16:11) and who is to be dethroned and "cast out" for ever.

Scripture thus gives depth to our understanding of the world around us. Indeed, unless we look at the unseen powers behind the material things we may readily be deceived.

This consideration may help us to understand better the passage in 1 Peter 3 alluded to above. There the apostle sets "the outward adorning (*kosmos*) of plaiting the hair, and of wearing jewels of gold, or of putting on apparel" in deliberate contrast with "the incorruptible apparel of a meek and quiet spirit, which is in the sight of God of great price." By inference, therefore, the former are corrupt and worthless to God. We may or may not be ready at once to accept Peter's

valuation, depending upon whether we see the
true import of his words. Here is what he is im-
plying. In the background behind these matters
of wearing apparel and jewelry and make-up,
there is a power at work for its own ends. Do not
let that power grip you.

What, we have to ask ourselves, is the motive
that activates us in relation to these things? It
may be nothing sensuous but altogether innocent, aiming by the use of tone and harmony and
perfect matching merely to gain an effect that is
aesthetically pleasing. There may be nothing intrinsically wrong in doing this; but do you and I
see what we are touching here? We are touching
that harmonious system behind the things seen,
a system that is controlled by God's enemy. So
let us be wary.

The Bible opens with God's creation of the
heavens and the earth. It does not say that he
created the world in the sense that we are dis-
cussing it now. Through the Bible the meaning
of "the world" undergoes a development, and it
is only in the New Testament (though perhaps to
a lesser extent already in the Psalms and some of
the Prophets) that "the world" comes to have its
full spiritual significance. We can readily see the
reason for this development. Before the Fall of
man, the world existed only in the sense of the
earth, the people on the earth, and the things on
the earth. As yet there was no *kosmos*, no
"world," in the sense of a constituted order.
With the Fall, however, Satan brought on to this
earth the order which he himself had conceived,
and with that began the world system of which

we are speaking. Originally our physical earth
had no connection with "the world" in this
sense of a Satanic system, nor indeed had man;
but Satan took advantage of man's sin, and of the
door this threw open to him, to introduce into
the earth the organization which he had set himself to establish. From that point of time this
earth was in "the world," and man was in "the
world." So we may say that before the Fall there
was an earth; after the Fall there was a "world";
at the Lord's return there will be a kingdom. Just
as the world belongs to Satan, so the Kingdom
belongs to our Lord Jesus. Moreover it is this
Kingdom that displaces and that will displace
the world. When the "Stone not made with
hands" shatters man's proud image, then the
kingdom of this world will "become the kingdom of our Lord and of his Christ" (Dan. 2:44,
45; Rev. 11:15).

Politics, education, literature, science, art,
law, commerce, music—such are the things that
constitute the *kosmos*, and these are things that
we meet daily. Subtract them and the world as a
coherent system ceases to be. In studying the history of mankind we have to acknowledge
marked progress in each of these departments.
The question however is: In what direction is
this "progress" tending? What is the ultimate
goal of all this development? At the end, John
tells us, antichrist will arise and will set up his
own kingdom in this world (1 John 2:18, 22; 4:3;
2 John 7; Rev. 13). *That* is the direction of this
world's advance. Satan is utilizing the material
world, the men of the world, the things that are

in the world, to head everything up eventually in the kingdom of antichrist. At that hour the world system will have reached its zenith; and at that hour every unit of it will be revealed to be anti-Christian.

In the book of Genesis we find in Eden no hint of technology, no mention of mechanical instruments. After the Fall, however, we read that among the sons of Cain there was a forger of cutting instruments of brass and iron. A few centuries ago it might have seemed fanciful to discern the spirit of antichrist in iron tools, even though for long the sword has been in open competition with the ploughshare. But today, in the hands of man, metals have been turned to sinister and deadly uses, and as the end approaches the widespread abuse of technology and engineering will become even more apparent.

The same thing applies to music and the arts. For the pipe and the harp seem also to have originated with the family of Cain, and today in unconsecrated hands their God-defying nature becomes increasingly clear. In many parts of the world it has long been easy to trace an intimate relationship between idolatry and the arts of painting, sculpture, and music. No doubt the day is coming when the nature of antichrist will be disclosed more openly than ever through song and dance and the visual and dramatic arts.

As for commerce, its connections are perhaps even more suspect. Satan was the first merchant, trading ideas with Eve for his own advantage, and in the figurative language of Ezekiel 28, which seems to reveal something of his original character, we read: "By thy traffic thou has increased thy riches, and thine heart is lifted up" (verse 5). Perhaps this does not have to be argued, for most of us will readily admit from experience the Satanic origin and nature of commerce. We shall say more of this later.

But what of education? Surely, we protest, that must be harmless. Anyway, our children have to be taught. But education, no less than commerce or technology, is one of the things of the world. It has its roots in the tree of knowledge. How earnestly, as Christians, we seek to protect our children from the world's more obvious snares. And yet it is quite true that we *have* to provide education for them. How are we going to solve the problem of letting them touch what is essentially a thing of the world, and at the same time guarding them from the great world system and its perils?

And what of science? It, too, is one of the units that constitute the *kosmos*. It, too, is knowledge. When we venture into the further reaches of science, and begin to speculate on the nature of the physical world—and of man—the question immediately arises: Up to what point is the pursuit of scientific research and discovery legitimate? Where is the line of demarcation between what is helpful and what is hurtful in the realm of knowledge? How can we pursue after knowledge and yet avoid being caught in Satan's meshes?

These, then, are the matters at which we must look. Oh, I know I shall appear to some to be overstating things, but this is necessary in order to drive home my point. For "if any man love the world, the love of the Father is not in him" (1 John 2:15). Ultimately, when we touch the things of the world, the question we must ask ourselves always is: "How is this thing affecting my relationship with the Father?"

The time has passed when we need to go out into the world in order to make contact with it. Today the world comes and searches us out. There is a force abroad now which is captivating men. Have you ever felt the power of the world as much as today? Have you ever heard so much talk about money? Have you ever thought so much about food and clothing? Wherever you go, even among Christians, the things of the world are the topics of conversation. The world has advanced to the very door of the Church and is seeking to draw even the saints of God into its grasp. Never in this sphere of things have we needed to know the power of the Cross of Christ to deliver us as we do at the present time.

Formerly we spoke much of sin and of the natural life. We could readily see the spiritual issues there, but we little realized then what equally great spiritual issues are at stake when we touch the world. There is a spiritual force behind this world scene which, by means of "the things that are in the world," is seeking to enmesh men in its system. It is not merely against sin therefore that the saints of God need to be on their guard, but against the ruler of this world. God is building up his Church to its consummation in the universal reign of Christ. Simultaneously his rival is building up this world system to its vain climax in the reign of antichrist. How watchful we need to be lest at any time we be found helping Satan in the construction of that ill-fated kingdom. When we are faced with alternatives and a choice of ways confronts us, the question is not: Is this good or evil? Is this helpful or hurtful? No, the question we must ask ourselves is: *Is it of this world, or of God?* For since there is only this one conflict in the universe, then whenever two conflicting courses lie open to us, the choice at issue is never a lesser one than: God ... or Satan?

2
The Trend Away from God

Having every one of us been in bondage to sin, we readily believe that sinful things are Satanic; but do we believe equally that the things of the world are Satanic? Many of us, I think, are still in two minds about this. Yet how clearly Scripture affirms that "the whole world lieth in the evil one" (1 John 5:19). Satan well knows that, generally speaking, to try to ensnare real Christians through things that are positively sinful is vain and futile. They will usually sense the danger and elude him. So he had contrived instead an

enticing network, the mesh of which is so skill-
fully woven as to entrap the most innocent of
men. We flee sinful lusts, and with good reason,
but when it comes to such seemingly innocuous
things as science and art and education, how
readily do we lose our sense of values and fall a
prey to his enticements!

Yet our Lord's sentence of judgment clearly
implies that everything that constitutes "the
world" is out of line with God's purpose. His
words, "Now is the judgment of this world,"
clearly imply the condemnation of all that goes
to make up the *kosmos,* and would never have
been uttered if there were not something radi-
cally amiss with it. Further, when Jesus goes on:
"Now shall the prince of this world be cast out,"
he is stressing not merely the intimate relation
between Satan and the world order but the fact
that its condemnation is linked with his. Do we
acknowledge that Satan is today the prince of
education and science and culture and the arts,
and that they, with him, are doomed? Do we acknowledge that he is the effective master of all
those things that together make up the world
system?

When mention is made of a dance hall or a
night club, our reaction as Christians is one of
instinctive disapproval. To us that is "the
world" *par excellence.* When, however, to go to
the other extreme, medical science or social service are discussed, there may be no such reaction
at all. These things command our tacit approval,
and maybe too our enthusiastic support. And between these extremes there lie a host of other

things varying widely in their influence for good or bad, between which we should probably none of us agree on where to draw an exact line. Yet let us face the fact that judgment has been pronounced by God, not upon certain selected things that belong to this world, but impartially upon them all.

Test yourself. If you venture into one of these approved fields, and then someone exclaims to you: "You have touched the world there," will you be moved? Probably not at all. It takes someone whom you really respect to say to you very straightly and earnestly: "Brother, you have become involved with Satan there!" before you will so much as hesitate. Is that not so? How would you feel if anyone said to you: "You have touched education there," or "You have touched medical science," or "You have touched commerce"? Would you react with the same degree of caution as you would if he had said, "You have touched the Devil there"? If we truly believed that whenever we touch any of these things that constitute the world we touch the prince of this world, then the awful seriousness of being in any wise involved in worldly things could not fail to strike home to us. "The whole world lieth in the evil one"—not a part of it, but *the whole.* Do not let us think for a moment that Satan opposes God only by means of sin and carnality in men's hearts; he opposes God by means of every worldly thing. Oh, I agree with you that the things of the world are all in one sense material, lifeless, intrinsically without power to harm us; yet even that should itself suggest that they are resistant to the purpose of God, as indeed is everything in which there is no touch of divine life.

The recurring phrase "after its kind" in Genesis 1 represents a law of reproduction that governs the whole realm of biological nature. It does not, however, govern the realm of the Spirit. For generation after generation, human parents can beget children after their kind; but one thing is certain: Christians cannot beget Christians! Not even where both parents are Christians will the children born to them automatically be Christians, no, not even in the first generation. It will take a fresh act of God every time.

And this principle applies no less truly in the affairs of mankind more widely. All that belongs to human nature continues spontaneously; all that belongs to God continues only for as long as God's working continues. And the world is all-inclusively that which can continue apart from divine activity, that is, which can go on by itself without the need of specific acts of God to maintain it in freshness. The world, and all that belongs to the world, does this naturally—it is its nature—and in doing so *it moves in a direction contrary to the will of God*. This statement we shall now seek to illustrate both from the Scripture and from Christian experience.

Let us take first the field of political science. The Old Testament history of Israel affords us the example of a highly privileged nation and its government. The people of Israel, we are told, wanted to be on terms with the nations around them, so they set their heart on a king. We will leave aside for the moment their election of Saul, and move on to the point where eventually, in his own time, God gave them the king of his choice who would establish the kingdom under his own direction.

Now even when this was clearly God's doing, the natural trend of the kingdom proved to be, "like the nations," away from him. For a kingdom is a worldly thing, and in keeping with all worldly things it tends to come into collision with the divine purpose. Wherever in the world a nation's government is left to itself, it follows its natural course which is further and further away from God. And what is true in secular national politics worked itself out equally surely even in divinely chosen Israel. Whenever God discontinued his specific acts on their behalf, the kingdom of Israel drifted into idolatrous political alignments. There were recoveries, it is true, but every one was marked by a definite divine intervention, and without such intervention the trend was always down hill.

It will scarcely surprise us that the same thing proves to be true in the field of commerce. I can think of no sphere where the temptation to dishonest and corrupt dealing is so great as here. We all know something of this. We all know how hard it is to remain straight and to conduct affairs honestly in the competitive world of trade. Many would say that it is impossible, and certainly to do so calls for a life that is cast upon God in an unusual way.

We recall that our Lord Jesus tells us of two

contrasting men, one who gained the whole world and forfeited his life, and another, a merchant, who went and sold all that he had to buy one priceless pearl. To the latter of these Jesus likened the kingdom of heaven (Matt. 16:26; 13:45, 46). The Spirit of God has not infrequently moved men in business to action of a like character. There have been not a few well-known business firms whose profits have been turned over to divine ends in the spread of the Gospel and in other ways.

I think of one such enterprise that, at the outset of its history, was the creation of a God-fearing business man. Now godly fear is a quality that can only exist as it is sustained from heaven, but business acumen and the efficient organization which it creates can be self-perpetuating. In the first generation of this firm's history we find divine life being mediated through its founder sufficient to hold what was even then a worldly concern securely under the authority of God. But by the second generation that restraint was gone and, as one would expect, the business gravitated automatically into the world system. Godly fear had drained away, but the firm itself is still flourishing.

Suppose we take now so apparently innocent a matter as agriculture. Here Genesis, written in a primitive world of flocks and husbandry, has something to tell us. After Adam's fall God was compelled to say to him, "Cursed is the ground for thy sake; in toil shalt thou eat of it all the days of thy life; thorns also and thistles shall it bring forth to thee; and thou shalt eat the herb of the field; in the sweat of thy face shalt thou eat bread, till thou return unto the ground." No one would suggest that in Eden, where the tree of life flourished, farming or gardening was wrong. It was God appointed. But as soon as it was let go from under the hand of God it deteriorated. Man was condemned to an endless round of drudgery and disappointment, and an element of perversity marked the fruit of his toil. The deliverance of Noah was God's great recovery movement, in which the earth was given a fresh start. But how swift, how tragic was man's reversion to type! "Noah began to be a husbandman, and planted a vineyard; and he drank of the wine, and was drunken; and he was uncovered within his tent." Of course agriculture is not in itself sinful, but here already its direction is away from God. Just let it follow its natural tendency and it will contrive to take a course diametrically opposed to him. Do we know something of this today in such physical disasters as the drying out of continents?

How different is the Church, God's husbandry! Through the grace of God and the indwelling Spirit she possesses an inherent life power capable, if she responds to it, of keeping her constantly moving Godward, or of recalling her Godward if she strays.

When we turn to education, both the Bible and experience have something to say to us. Speaking allegorically we might say that in rejecting Saul and choosing David God was passing over a man distinguished by his head (for he was that much taller than his peers) in favor of the man after his heart! But more seriously, the men such as Joseph and Moses and Daniel, of whose wisdom God made public use, each received in a direct way from God himself the understanding they needed. They took little account of their secular education. And the apostle Paul clearly placed scholarship among the "all things" that he counted to be loss for the excellency of the knowledge of Christ Jesus his Lord (Phil. 3:8). He draws a clear distinction between the wisdom of the world and the wisdom that comes from God (1 Cor. 1:21, 30).

But it is experience that demonstrates the essential worldliness of scholarship as such. Most of the historic university colleges of the West were founded by Christian men with a desire to provide their fellows with a good education under Christian influence. During their founders' lifetimes the tone of those foundations was high, because these men put real spiritual content into them. When, however, the men themselves passed away, the spiritual control passed away too, and education followed its inevitable course toward the world of materialism and away from God. In some cases it may have taken a long time, for religious tradition dies hard; but the tendency has always been obvious, and in most cases the destination has by now been reached. When material things are under spiritual control they fulfill their proper subordinate role. Released from that restraint they manifest very quickly the power that lies behind them. The law of their nature asserts itself, and their worldly character is proved by the course they take.

The spread of missionary enterprise in our present era gives us an opportunity to test this principle in the religious institutions of our day and of our land. Over a century ago the Church set out to establish in China schools and hospitals with a definite spiritual tone and an evangelistic objective. In those early days not much importance was attached to the buildings, while considerable emphasis was placed on the institutions' role in the proclamation of the Gospel. Ten or fifteen years ago you could go over the same ground and in many places find much larger and finer institutions on those original sites, but compared with the earlier years, far fewer converts. And by today many of those splendid schools and colleges have become purely educational centers, lacking in any truly evangelistic motive at all, while to an almost equal extent, many of the hospitals exist now solely as places merely of physical and no longer of spiritual healing. The men who initiated them had, by their close walk with God, held those institutions steadfastly into his purpose; but when they passed away, the institutions themselves quickly gravitated toward worldly standards and goals, and in doing so classified themselves as "things of the world." We should not be surprised that this is so.

In the early chapters of the Acts we read how a contingency arose which led the Church to institute relief for the poorer saints. That urgent institution of social service was clearly blessed of God, but it was of a temporary nature. Do you exclaim, "How good if it had continued!"? Only

one who does not know God would say that. Had
those relief measures been prolonged indefinitely they would certainly have veered in the
direction of the world, once the spiritual influence at work in their inception was removed. It
is inevitable.

For there is a distinction between the Church
of God's building, on the one hand, and on the
other, those valuable social and charitable by-
products that are thrown off by it from time to
time through the faith and vision of its members.
The latter, for all their origin in spiritual vision,
possess in themselves a power of independent
survival which the Church of God does not have.
They are works which the faith of God's children
may initiate and pioneer, but which, once the
way has been shown and the professional standard set, can be readily sustained or imitated by
men of the world quite apart from that faith.

The Church of God, let me repeat, never ceases
to be dependent upon the life of God for its main-
tenance. Imagine a living church in a city today
with its fellowship and prayer and Gospel witness, and its many homes and centers of spiritual
activity. Some years hence what do we find? If
God's people have followed him in faith and
obedience it may be a place filled more than ever
with the life and light of the Lord and the power
of his Word; but if in unfaithfulness to him they
have forsaken their vision of Christ, it may
equally well have become a place where people
preach atheism. By then as a church it will have
ceased to exist. For the Church depends for its
very existence upon a ceaseless impartation of

fresh life from God, and cannot survive one day without it.

But suppose alongside that church there is a school or hospital or publishing house, or other religiously founded institution, originating in the faith of the same church members. Assuming that the need for its service continues still to exist ten years hence and has not been met by some alternative private or State enterprise, then the probability is that that work will still be operating then at a no less efficient and commendable standard of service. For given ordinary administrative know-how, a college or a hospital can continue efficiently on a purely institutional level without any fresh influx of divine life. The vision may have gone, but the establishment carries on indefinitely. It has become no less worldly than everything else that can be maintained apart from the life of God. And every such thing is embraced in the Lord's sentence: "Now is the judgment of this world."

Suppose I put to you the question, "What work are you engaged in?" You answer, "Medical work." You say that without any special consciousness other than pride in the compassionate nature of your calling, and without any sense of the possible danger of your situation. But if I tell you that medical science is one more unit of a system that is Satan-controlled, what then? Assuming that as a Christian you take me seriously, then you are at once alarmed, and your reaction may even be to wonder if you had not better quit your profession. No, do not cease being a doctor! But walk softly, for you are upon territory that is governed by God's enemy, and unless you are on the watch you are as liable as anyone else to fall a prey to his devices.

Or suppose you are engineering, or farming, or publishing. Take heed, for these too are things of the world, just as much as running a place of entertainment or a haunt of vice. Unless you tread softly you will be caught up somewhere in Satan's snares and will lose the liberty that is yours as a child of God.

How then, you ask, are we to be delivered from his entanglements? Many think that to escape the world is a matter of consecration, of dedicating themselves anew and more wholeheartedly to the things of God. No, it is a matter of salvation. By nature we are all entrapped in that Satanic system, and we have no escape apart from the mercy of the Lord. All our consecration is powerless to deliver us; we are dependent upon his compassion and upon his redemptive work alone to save us out of it. He is well able to do so, and the means whereby he does it will be the theme of our next chapter. God can set us upon a rock and keep our feet from slipping. Helped by him we may turn our trade or profession to the service of his will for as long as he desires it.

But let me repeat again that the natural trend of all the "things that are in the world" is toward Satan and away from God. Some of them may have been set going by men of the Spirit with a goal that is Godward, but as soon as the restraint of the divine life is removed from them, they automatically swerve around and take that other direction. No wonder then that Satan's eyes are ever on the world's end, and on the prospect that at that time all the things of the world will revert to him. Even now, and all the time, they are moving in his direction, and at the end time they may be expected to have reached their goal. As we touch any one of the units of his system, this thought should give us pause, lest we be found inadvertently helping to construct his kingdom.

3
A World Under Water

"Go ye into all the world, and preach the gospel to the whole creation. He that believeth and is baptized shall be saved; but he that disbelieveth shall be condemned" (Mark 16:15, 16).

To many of us the form of that second sentence comes as a surprise. Jesus did not say that he who believes and is saved shall be baptized. No, he put it the other way round. He who believes and is baptized, he said, shall be saved. It is only at our peril that we change something that the Lord has said into something that he did not say.

Everything he says matters, and he means every word of it. But if this is so, then it must be a fact that only by having faith in him and being baptized are we saved. Some will be puzzled at this. What do you mean? they will protest. But do not puzzle; and do not blame me! *I* did not say that; my Lord said it. He it was who laid down the order: faith, then baptism, then salvation. We must not reverse it to faith, salvation, baptism, however much we might prefer it that way. What the Lord said must stand, and it is for us only to pay heed to it.

(I make no apology for taking these words of Mark 16:16 as authentic words of Jesus, though I am aware that there are critics who question them. Once in a country village I came across a tailor named Chen. He had picked up a Gospel of Mark, and when he reached this passage which the critics all affirm does not belong to that Gospel at all, he believed and trusted in the Lord. There were no other Christians in the place and so no one to baptize him. What should he do? Then he read verse 20. God himself would confirm to him his word: that was sufficient. So in his simplicity he decided to test out one of the promises in verse 18. Accordingly he visited several neighbors who were sick. After prayer, he laid hands on them in Jesus' name and then returned home. In due course and without exception, he told me, they recovered. That satisfied him. With his faith confirmed he carried quietly on with his tailoring, where, when I came across him, he was faithfully witnessing to his Lord. If *he* could take God's word seriously, must not I?)

So I repeat, "He that believeth and is baptized shall be saved." Do you mean to tell me, you will now exclaim, that you believe in baptismal regeneration? No, indeed I do not! The Lord did not say, "Believe and be baptized and thou shalt be born again"; and since he did not say that, I have no need to believe in that. His words are: "He that believeth and is baptized *shall be saved.*" What therefore I do believe in is baptismal salvation.

So the question naturally arises: What does this statement *mean?* And what does it mean when Luke tells us that, in response to Peter's exhortation to *"save yourselves* from this crooked generation," then they that received his word *were baptized?*

To answer this we must ask ourselves first what we mean by the word "saved." I am afraid we have a very wrong idea of salvation. All that most of us know about salvation is that we shall be saved from hell and into heaven; or alternatively, that we are saved from our sins to live henceforth a holy life. But we are wrong. In Scripture we find that salvation goes further than that. For it is concerned not so much with sin and hell, or holiness and heaven, but with something else.

We know that every good gift that God offers to us is given to meet and counter a contrasting evil. He gives us justification because there is condemnation. He gives us eternal life because there is death. He offers us forgiveness because there are sins. He brings us salvation—because of what? Justification is in terms of condemnation, heaven is in terms of hell, forgiveness is in relation to sins. Then to what is salvation related? Salvation, we shall see, is related to the *kosmos*, the world.

Satan is the personal enemy of Christ. He works through the flesh of man to produce this pattern of things on the earth in which we have all become involved; not one of us is exempt. And this whole cosmic pattern is peculiarly at odds with God the Father. I think we all know how the three dark forces, the world, the flesh and the devil, stand in opposition to the three divine persons. The flesh is ranged against the Holy Spirit as Paraclete, Satan himself against Christ Jesus as Lord, and the world against the Father as Creator.

What we are speaking of as the *kosmos* always stands opposed to God as Father and Originator. His was the eternal plan in creation hinted at in the words "It was very good," a plan toward which he has not ceased to work. From before the foundation of the world he had purposed in his heart to have on earth an order of which mankind would be the pinnacle and which should freely display the character of his Son. But Satan intervened. Using this earth as his springboard and man as his tool, he usurped God's creation to make of it instead something centered in himself and reflecting his own image. Thus this alien system of things was a direct challenge to the divine plan.

So today we are confronted by two worlds, two spheres of authority, having two totally different and opposed characters. For me now it is no

mere matter of a future heaven and hell; it is a
question of these two worlds today, and of
whether I belong to an order of things of which
Christ is sovereign Lord, or to an opposed order
of things having Satan as its effective head.

Thus salvation is not so much a personal question of sins forgiven or of hell avoided. It is to be
seen rather in terms of a system from which we
come out. When I am saved, I make my exodus
out of one whole world and my entry into another. I am saved *now* out of that whole or-
ganized realm which Satan has constructed in
defiance of the purpose of God.

That realm, that all-embracing *kosmos*, has
many strange facets. Sin of course has its prior
place there, and worldly lusts; but no less part of
it are our more estimable human standards and
ways of doing things. The human mind, its culture and its philosophies, all are included, together with all the very best of humanity's social
and political ideologies. Alongside these too we
should doubtless place the world's religions,
and among them those speckled birds, worldly
Christianity and its "world Church." Wherever
the power of natural man dominates, there you
have an element in that system which is under
the direct inspiration of Satan.

If that is the world, what then is salvation?
Salvation means that I escape from that. I go out,
I make an exit from that all-embracing *kosmos*. I
belong no more to Satan's pattern of things. I set
my heart on that upon which God's heart is set. I
take as my goal his eternal purpose in Christ, and
I step into that and am delivered from this.

He that believeth and is baptized shall be saved. What Jesus said he plainly means. I take that step of faith: I believe and am baptized, and I come out a saved man. *That* is salvation. So never let us regard baptism as of small concern. Tremendous things hang upon it. It is no less a question than of two violently opposing worlds and of our translation from the one into the other.

There is in Scripture another passage which brings baptism and salvation together to illustrate this theme. I allude to Chapter 3 of 1 Peter. There the apostle tells us how "the longsuffering of God waited in the days of Noah, while the ark was a preparing, wherein few, that is, eight souls, were saved through water" (verse 20). The water, he says, is a figure or likeness, or (as the R.V. margin reads) an antitype, of something else. "Which also in the antitype doth now save you, even baptism." So baptism, he reasons, saves us *now*. Clearly Peter believed in our salvation through baptism as firmly as he believed in Noah's salvation through water. Please remember, I am not saying regeneration, and I am not saying deliverance from hell or from sin. Understand clearly that we are talking here about salvation. It is not just a question of terms; it concerns our being fundamentally severed from today's world system.

To understand better what Peter means we should turn back to his source in Chapters 6 to 8 of Genesis. The picture is instructive. There in Noah's day we find a wholly corrupt world. Created first by God, the earth had become corrupted by man's act on that day when he placed himself under Satan. Sin, once introduced, had developed and run riot, until even God's Holy Spirit cried Enough! Things had reached a state where they could never be remedied; they could only be judged and removed.

So God commanded Noah to build an ark, and to bring his family and the creatures into it, and then the flood came. By it they were "lifted up above the earth" upon waters that covered "all the high mountains that were under the whole heaven." Every living thing, both man and beast, perished and those only who rode the waters in the ark were saved. The significant thing here is not just that they escaped death by drowning. That is not the point. The real point for us is that they were the only people to come out from that corrupt system of things, that world under water. Personal life is the inevitable consequence of coming out, personal perdition of staying in, but salvation is the coming out itself, not the effect of it. Note this difference for it is a great one. Salvation is essentially a present exit from a doomed order which is Satan's.

Praise God, they came out! How? Through the waters. So today when believers are baptized they go symbolically through water, just as Noah passed in the ark through the waters of the flood. And this passage through water signifies their escape from the world, their exodus from the system of things that, with its prince, is under the divine sentence. May I say this especially to those who are being baptized today.[1] Please re-

[1] The occasion of this address was a baptismal service in London in the month of May 1939.

member, you are not the only one who is in the water. As you step down into the water, a whole world goes down with you. When you come up, you come up in Christ, in the ark that rides the waves, but your world stays behind. For you, that world is submerged, drowned like Noah's, put to death in the death of Christ and never to be revived. It is by baptism that you declare this. "Lord, I leave my world behind. Thy Cross separates me from it for ever!"

Speaking figuratively, therefore, when you go through the waters of baptism everything belonging to the former system of things is cut off by those waters never to return. You alone emerge. For you it is a passage into another world, a world where you will find a dove and the fresh leaves of olive trees. You go out of the world that is under judgment, into a world that is marked by newness of divine life.

I want to emphasize again that you were not the only one that went down into the water; your world went down with you. And there it stayed. From the standpoint of your new situation you will find that the water always covers the world to which you belonged before. The same flood which saved Noah and his family drowned the world in which they had once lived their lives—the very same flood. So the same water on the one hand puts you and me on salvation ground in Christ, and on the other hand buries Satan's whole system of things. Not only does your own history as a child of Adam end in your baptism; your world also ends there. In both cases it is a death and a burial with nothing resurrected. It is an end of everything.

This means that you cannot carry over anything from that former world into the new one. What belonged to that former realm of things in Adam stays there and may never be recalled. Formerly perhaps you were an employee in a shop, or a servant in a house. Or perhaps you were the master, or the manager, or director of a business. Still today you may be a master, or still a servant, but you will find that when coming to divine things, when coming to the Church of God and the service of God, there is neither bond nor free, neither employer nor employee. Again you may be a Jew or a Gentile, or any of a hundred-and-one things that were of repute—or of disrepute—in Adam. When you pass through this water, all that system of things goes, never to return. Instead you see yourself in Christ, where there is neither Jew nor Greek, barbarian nor Scythian nor anything else, but one new man. You have entered an order of things characterized by olive trees and olive leaves, whose secret is divine life. The expression "through the resurrection of Jesus Christ" colors the whole future (1 Pet. 3:21). It implies that you have passed into something altogether new which God is creating. According to commentators (Robert Young *Analytical Concordance of the Holy Bible*), the very name Ararat means "Holy Ground." Be that as it may, we praise God that the ark which rested on that renewed earth was filled with creatures, typifying a new creation. Out of the death of Christ God brings into being an entire new creation, and in union with Christ risen he is introducing man into that. In Christ, you and I are there!

You ask me now whether it matters if we are not baptized. My only answer is that the Lord himself commanded it (Matt. 28:19). And it was a step from which he himself refused to be dissuaded (Matt. 3:13-15). Peter describes baptism as the appeal, or testimony, of a good conscience towards God (verse 21). A testimony is a declaration. So through this act you say something, you declare where you stand, perhaps without using words but certainly by what you do. Passing through the water you proclaim to the whole universe that you have left your world behind and have entered into something utterly new. That is salvation. You take a public stand where God has placed you in Christ.

This helps to explain why in Scripture we find passages concerning salvation which are hard to interpret if we relate salvation only to hell or to sin. It illumines, for instance, the apparently difficult words of Paul and Silas to the jailor at Philippi. The man asked, "What must I do to be saved?" What will your answer be? If you are a sound evangelical preacher in the present day, you will say with assurance, "Believe on the Lord Jesus Christ, and thou shalt be saved." But Paul in fact added: "thou and thy house." Do you really mean to say, I can hear you exclaim, that if I believe on the Lord Jesus, both I and my family will be saved? Now once again we must be careful. Paul did not say, Believe on the Lord Jesus and thou and thy house will have eternal life. He said, "Believe on the Lord Jesus Christ, and thou shalt *be saved*, thou and thy house." Remember, he is concerned with a system of things, and with the jailor's repudiation of and exit from that system. When, as head of his family, that man makes the declaration that from that day forward he and his house are going to serve the Lord, and when that declaration becomes publicly known, even people passing through the street will point in the door and say, "They are Christian folk."

That is what it means to be saved. You declare that you belong to another system of things. People point to you and say, "Oh, yes, that is a Christian family; they belong to the Lord!" That is the salvation which the Lord desires for you, that by your public testimony you declare before God, "My world has gone; I am entering into another." May the Lord give us that kind of salvation, to find ourselves uprooted entire out of the old, doomed order of things and firmly planted in the new, divine one.

For, praise God, there is a glorious positive side to all this. We are saved "through the resurrection of Jesus Christ, who," Peter goes on to say, "is on the right hand of God, having gone into heaven, angels and authorities and powers being made subject unto him" (verse 22). God has set his Son supreme above everything, and made all authorities his subjects. A God who can do this is well able to bring me, body and soul, into that other realm.

So, to recapitulate, we have here two worlds. On the one hand there is the world in Adam, held fast in bondage to Satan; on the other hand there is the new creation in Christ, the sphere of activity of God's Holy Spirit. How do you and I get out of the one sphere, Adam, into the other

sphere, Christ? If you are uncertain how to answer that question, may I ask you another? How
did you get into Adam in the first place? For the
way of entry indicates the way out. You entered
the sphere of Adam by being born into Adam's
race. How then do you get out? Obviously by
death. And how, in turn, do you enter the sphere
of Christ? The answer is the same: by birth. The
way of entry into the family of God is by new
birth to a living hope, through the resurrection of
Jesus Christ from the dead (1 Pet. 1:3). Having
become united with him by the likeness of his
death, you are united with him also by the likeness of his resurrection (Rom. 6:5). Death puts an
end to your relationship with the old world, and
resurrection brings you into living touch with
this new one.

Finally, what occupies the gap? What is the
steppingstone between those two worlds? Is it
not burial? "We were buried therefore with him
through baptism into death" (Rom. 6:4). From
one point of view there is a grim finality about
those words "buried into death." My history in
Adam has already been concluded in the death
of Christ, so that when I walk away from that
burial I can say I am a "finished" man. But I can
say more, for, praise God, it is no less true that
there is the other side. Since "Christ was raised
from the dead," when I come out of the water
and walk away, I may walk "in newness of life"
(6:4).

This double outcome of the Cross is implied
too in the preceding words of Romans 6:3. "Are
ye ignorant that all we who were baptized into

Christ Jesus were baptized into his death?" Here in a single sentence the two aspects of baptism are again hinted at. It is baptism into two things. First, we who believe were "baptized *into his death.*" This is a tremendous fact, but is it all? Not by any means, for in the second place the same verse says that we were "baptized *into Christ Jesus.*" A baptism into the death of Christ ends my relation with this world, but a baptism into Christ Jesus as a living Person, Head of a new race, opens up for me a new world of things altogether. Going into the water I simply act the whole thing out, affirming publicly that the "judgment of this world" became real to me from the day when the "lifted up" Son of man drew me to himself.

What a Gospel to preach to the whole creation!

4
Crucified Unto Me

Separation to God, separation from the world, is the first principle of Christian living. John, in his revelation of Jesus Christ, was shown two irreconcilable extremes, two worlds that morally were poles apart. He was first carried away in the Spirit into a wilderness to see Babylon, mother of the harlots and of the abominations of the earth (17:3). Then he was carried in the same Spirit to a great and high mountain, from whence to view Jerusalem, the bride, the Lamb's wife (21:10). The contrast is clear and could hardly be more explicitly stated.

Whether we be a Moses or a Balaam, in order to have God's view of things we must be taken like John to a mountaintop. Many cannot see God's eternal plan, or if they see it they understand it only as dry-as-dust doctrine, but they are content to stay on the plains. For understanding never moves us; only revelation does that. From the wilderness we may see something of Babylon, but we need spiritual revelation to see God's new Jerusalem. Once see it, and we shall never be the same again. As Christians therefore we bank everything on that opening of the eyes, but to experience it we must be prepared to forsake the common levels and climb.

The harlot Babylon is always "the great city" (16:19, etc.) with the emphasis on her attainment of greatness. The bride Jerusalem is by contrast "the holy city" (21:2, 10) with the accent correspondingly on her separation to God. She is "from God," and is prepared "for her husband." For this reason she possesses the glory of God. This is a matter of experience for us all. Holiness in us is what is of God, what is wholly set apart to Christ. It follows the rule that only what originated in heaven returns there; for nothing else is holy. Let go this principle of holiness and we are instantly in Babylon.

Thus it comes about that the wall is the first feature John mentions in his description of the city itself. There are gates, making provision for the goings of God, but the wall takes precedence. For, I repeat, separation is the first principle of Christian living. If God wants his city with its measurements and its glory in that day, then we must build that wall in human hearts now. This means in practice that we must guard as precious all that is of God and refuse and reject all that is of Babylon. I do not imply by this a separation between Christians. We dare not exclude our brethren themselves, even when we cannot take part in some of the things they do. No, we must love and receive our fellow Christians, but be uncompromising in our separation from the world in principle.

Nehemiah in his day succeeded in rebuilding the wall of Jerusalem, but only in the face of great opposition. For Satan hates distinctiveness. Separation of men to God he cannot abide. Nehemiah and his colleagues armed themselves therefore, and thus equipped for war they laid stone to stone. This is the price of holiness we must be prepared for.

For build we certainly must. Eden was a garden without artificial wall to keep foes out; so that Satan had entry. God intended that Adam and Eve should "guard it" (Gen. 2:15) by themselves constituting a moral barrier to him. Today, through Christ, God plans in the heart of his redeemed people an Eden to which, in triumphant fact, Satan will at last have no moral access whatever. "There shall in no wise enter into it anything unclean, or he that maketh an abomination and a lie; but only they which are in the Lamb's book of life."

Most of us would agree that to the apostle Paul was given a special revelation of the Church of God. In a similar way we feel that God gave to

John a special understanding of the nature of the world. *Kosmos* is in fact peculiarly John's word. The other Gospels use it only fifteen times (Matthew nine, Mark and Luke three each) while Paul has it forty-seven times in eight letters. But John uses it 105 times in all, seventy-eight in his Gospel, twenty-four in his epistles and a further three in the Revelation.

In his first epistle John writes: "All that is in the world, the lust of the flesh, and the lust of the eyes, and the vainglory of life, is not of the Father, but is of the world" (2:16). In these words that so clearly reflect the temptation of Eve (Gen. 3:6) John defines the things of the world. All that can be included under lust or primitive desire, all that excites greedy ambition, and all that arouses in us the pride or glamor of life, all such things are part of the Satanic system. Perhaps we scarcely need stay here to consider further the first two of these, but let us look for a moment at the third. Everything that stirs pride in us is of the world. Prominence, wealth, achievement, these the world acclaim. Men are justly proud of success. Yet John labels all that brings this sense of success as "of the world."

Every success therefore that we experience (and I am not suggesting that we should be failures!) calls in us for an instant, humble confession of its inherent sinfulness, for whenever we meet success we have in some degree touched the world system. Whenever we sense complacency over some achievement we may know at once that we have touched the world. We may know, too, that we have brought ourselves under the judgment of God, for have we not already agreed that the whole world is under judgment? Now (and let us try to grasp this fact) those who realize this and confess their need are thereby safeguarded.

But the trouble is, how many of us are aware of it? Even those of us who live our lives in the seclusion of our own private homes are just as prone to fall a prey to the pride of life as those who have great public successes. A woman in a humble kitchen can touch the world and its complacency even while cooking the daily meal or entertaining guests. Every glory that is not glory to God is vainglory, and it is amazing what paltry successes can produce vainglory. Wherever we meet pride we meet the world, and there is an immediate leakage in our fellowship with God. Oh that God would open our eyes to see clearly what the world is! Not only evil things, but all those things that draw us ever so gently away from God, are units of that system that is antagonistic to him. Satisfaction in the achievement of some legitimate piece of work has the power to come instantly between us and God himself. For if it is the pride of life and not the praise of God that it awakens in us, we can know for certain that we have touched the world. There is thus a constant need for us to watch and pray if we are to maintain our communion with God unsullied.

What then is the way of escape from this snare which the Devil has set to catch God's people? First let me say emphatically that it is not to be found by our running away. Many think we can escape the world by seeking to abstain from the things of the world. That is folly. How could we ever escape the world system by using what, after all, are little more than worldly methods? Let me remind you of Jesus' words in Matt. 11:18, 19. "John came neither eating nor drinking, and they say, 'He hath a devil.' The Son of man came eating and drinking, and they say, 'Behold, a gluttonous man, and a winebibber, a friend of publicans and sinners!' " Some think that John the Baptist here offers us a recipe for escape from the world, but "neither eating nor drinking" is not Christianity. Christ came both eating and drinking, and that *is* Christianity! The apostle Paul speaks of "the elements of the world," and he defines these as, "handle not, nor taste, nor touch" (Col. 2:20, 21). So abstinence is merely worldly and no more, and what hope is there, by using worldly elements, of escaping the world system? Yet how many earnest Christians are forsaking all sorts of worldly pleasures in the hope thereby of being delivered out of the world! You can build yourself a hermit's hut in some remote spot and think to escape the world by retiring there, but the world will follow you even as far as that. It will dog your footsteps and find you out no matter where you hide.

Our deliverance from the world begins, not with our giving up this or that but with our seeing, as with God's eyes, that it is a world under sentence of death as in the figure with which we opened this chapter, "Fallen, fallen is Babylon the great!" (Rev. 18:2). Now a sentence of death is always passed, not on the dead but on the living. And in one sense the world is a living force today, relentlessly pursuing and seeking out its subjects. But while it is true that when sentence is pronounced death lies still in the future, it is nevertheless certain. A person under sentence of death *has* no future beyond the confines of a condemned cell. Likewise the world, being under sentence, has no future. The world system has not yet been "wound up," as we say, and terminated by God, but the winding up is a settled matter. It makes all the difference to us that we *see* this. Some folk seek deliverance from the world in asceticism, and like the Baptist, neither eat nor drink. That today is Buddhism, not Christianity. As Christians we both eat and drink, but we do so in the realization that eating and drinking belong to the world and, with it, are under the death sentence, so they have no grip upon us.

Let us suppose that the municipal authorities of Shanghai should decree that the school where you are employed must be closed. As soon as you hear this news you realize there is no future for you in that school. You go on working there for a period, but you do not build up anything for the future there. Your attitude to the school changes the instant you hear it must close down. Or to use another illustration, suppose the government decides to close a certain bank. Will you hasten to deposit in it a large sum of money in order to save the bank from collapse? No, not a cent more do you pay into it once you hear it has no future. You put nothing in because you expect nothing from it.

And we may justly say of the world that it is under a decree of closure. Babylon fell when her champions made war with the Lamb, and when by his death and resurrection he overcame them, who is Lord of lords and King of kings (Rev. 17:14). There is no future for her.

A revelation of the Cross of Christ involves for us the discovery of this fact, that through it everything belonging to the world is under sentence of death. We still go on living in the world and using the things of the world, but we can build no future with them, for the Cross has shattered all our hope in them. The Cross of our Lord Jesus, we may truly say, has ruined our prospects in the world; we have nothing to live for there.

There is no true way of salvation from the world that does not start from such a revelation. We need only try to escape the world by running away from it to discover how much we love it, and how much it loves us. We may flee where we will to avoid it, but it will assuredly track us down. But we inevitably lose all interest in the world, and it loses its grip on us, as soon as it dawns upon us that the world is doomed. To see that is to be automatically severed from Satan's entire economy.

At the end of his letter to the Galatians Paul states this very clearly. "Far be it from me to glory, save in the cross of our Lord Jesus Christ, through which the world hath been crucified unto me, and I unto the world" (6:14). Have you noticed something striking about this verse? In relation to the world it speaks of the two aspects of the work of the Cross already hinted at in our last chapter. "I have been crucified unto the world" is a statement which we find fairly easy to fit into our understanding of being crucified with Christ as defined in such passages as Romans 6. But here it specifically says too that "the world has been crucified to me." When God comes to you and me with the revelation of the finished work of Christ, he not only shows us ourselves there on the Cross. He shows us our world there too. If you and I cannot escape the judgment of the Cross, then neither can the world escape the judgment of the Cross. Have I really seen this? That is the question. When I see it, then I do not try to repudiate a world I love; I see that the Cross *has* repudiated it. I do not try to escape a world that clings to me; I see that by the Cross I *have* escaped.

Like so much else in the Christian life, the way of deliverance out of the world comes as a surprise to most of us, for it is so at odds with all man's natural concepts. Man seeks to solve the problem of the world by removing himself physically from what he regards as the danger zone. But physical separation does not bring about spiritual separation; and the reverse is also true, that physical contact with the world does not necessitate spiritual capture by the world. Spiritual bondage to the world is a fruit of spiritual blindness, and deliverance is the outcome of having our eyes opened. However close our touch with the world may be outwardly, we are released from its power when we truly see its nature. The essential character of the world is

Satanic; it is at enmity with God. To see this is to find deliverance.

Let me ask you: What is your occupation? A merchant? A doctor? Do not run away from these callings. Simply write down: Trade is under the sentence of death. Write: Medicine is under the sentence of death. If you do that in truth, life will be changed for you hereafter. In the midst of a world under judgment for its hostility to God you will know what it is to live as one who truly loves and fears him.

5
Distinctiveness

May I now invite your attention to words Jesus addressed to the Jews in John 8:23. "Ye are from beneath; I am from above: ye are of this world; I am not of this world." I wish us to note especially here the use of the words "from" and "of." The Greek word in each case is *ek*, which means "out of" and implies origin. *Ek tou kosmos* is the expression used: "from, or of, or out of, this world." So the sense of the passage is: "Your place of origin is beneath; my place of origin is above. Your place of origin is this world; my

place of origin is not this world." The question is
not: Are you a good or a bad person? but, What is
your place of origin? We do not ask, Is this thing
right? or, Is that thing wrong? but, Where did it
originate? It is origin that determines everything. "That which is born of the flesh is flesh:
that which is born of the Spirit is spirit" (John
3:6).

So when Jesus turns to his disciples he can
say, using the same Greek preposition, "If ye
were of the world (*ek tou kosmos*), the world
would love its own: but because ye are not of the
world, but I chose you out of the world, therefore
the world hateth you" (John 15:19). Here we
have the same expression, "not of the world,"
but in addition we have another and more force-
ful expression, "I chose you out of the world." In
this latter instance there is a double emphasis.
As before there is an *ek*, "out of," but in addition
to this the verb "to choose," *eklego*, itself contains another *ek*. Jesus is saying that his disciples
have been "chosen-out, out of the world."

There is this double *ek* in the life of every believer. Out of that vast organization called the
kosmos, out of all the great mass of individuals
belonging to it and involved in it, out, clean out
of all of that, God has called us. Thence comes
the title "Church," *ekklesia*, God's "called-out
ones." From the midst of the great *kosmos* God
calls one here and one there; and all whom he
calls he calls out. There is no such thing as a call
from God that is not a call "out of" the world.
The church is *ekklesia*. In the divine intention
there is no *klesia* which lacks the *ek*.

If you are a called one, then you are a called-out one. If God has called you at all then he has called you to live in spirit outside the world system. Originally we were in that Satanic system with no way of escape; but we were called, and that calling brought us out. True, that statement is a negative one, but there is a positive side also to our constitution; for as the people of God we have two titles, each of them significant according to the way we view ourselves. If we look back at our past history we are *ekklesia*, the Church; but if we look to our present life in God we are the Body of Christ, the expression on earth of him who is in heaven. From the standpoint of God's choice of us we are "out of" the world; but from the standpoint of our new life we are not of the world at all, but from above. On the one hand we are a chosen people, called and delivered out of the world system. On the other we are a regenerate people, utterly unrelated to that system because by the Spirit we are born from above. So John sees the holy city coming down "out of heaven from God" (Rev. 21:10). As the people of God, heaven is not only our destiny but our origin.

This is an amazing thing, that in you and me there is an element that is essentially otherworldly. So otherworldly is it indeed that no matter how this world may progress, it can never advance one step in likeness to that. The life we have as God's gift came from heaven and never was in the world at all. It has no correspondence with the world but is in perfect correspondence with heaven; and though we must mingle with the world daily, it will never let us settle down and feel at home there.

Let us consider for a moment this divine gift, this life of Christ indwelling the heart of regenerate man. The apostle Paul has a great deal to say about this. In an illuminating passage in 1 Corinthians he makes a striking twofold statement: (a) that God himself has placed us in Christ, and (b) that Christ has been "made unto us wisdom from God: righteousness and sanctification and redemption" (1:30). Here are examples of the whole range of human need that God has met in his Son. We have shown elsewhere[1] how God does not distribute to us these qualities of righteousness, holiness and so on in installments "to be taken as required." What he does is to give us Christ as the inclusive answer to all our needs. He makes his Son to be my righteousness and my holiness, and everything else I lack, on the ground that he has already placed me in Christ crucified and risen.

Now I would draw your attention to the last word, "redemption." For redemption has a great deal to do with the world. The Israelites, you will recall, were "redeemed" out of Egypt, which at that time was all the world they knew, and which is for us a figure of this world under Satanic rule. "I am Jehovah," God said to Israel, "and I will redeem you with a stretched out arm." So God brought them out, setting a barrier of judgment between them and Pharaoh's pursuing host, so that Moses could sing of Israel as

[1]*The Normal Christian Life*, London, 1961, pp. 127 f.

"the people which thou has redeemed" (Exod. 6:6; 15:13).

In the light of this, let us now take Paul's double statement. If (a) *God has placed us in Christ*, then since Christ is altogether out of the world, we too are altogether out of the world. He is now our sphere, and being in him, we are by definition out of that other sphere. The Father "delivered us out of the power of darkness, and translated us into the kingdom of his dear Son; *in whom we have our redemption*" (Col. 1:13, 14, A.V.). This transfer was the subject of our last two chapters.

Furthermore, if also (b) *Christ is "made unto us redemption"*—if that is to say, he is given to us to be that—then that means that *within us* God has set Christ himself as the barrier to resist the world. I have met many young Christians trying to resist the world, trying in one way or another to live an unworldly life. They found it very hard and, moreover, such effort is of course wholly unnecessary. For by his own essential "otherness" Christ is our barrier to the world, and we need nothing more. It is not that we must do anything in relation to our redemption, any more than the people of Israel did anything in relation to theirs. They simply trusted in God's redeeming arm outstretched on their behalf. And Christ *is made* to us redemption. In my heart there is a barrier set up between me and the world, the barrier of another kind of life, namely that of my Lord himself, and God has set the barrier there. And because of Christ, the world cannot reach me.

What need therefore have I to try either to resist or to escape the system of things? If I look within myself for something with which to meet and overcome the world, I instantly find everything within me crying out *for* that world, while if I struggle to detach myself from it I simply become more and more involved. But let the day once come when I recognize that within me Christ is my redemption, and that in him I *am* altogether "out." That day will see the end of struggling. I shall simply tell him that I can do nothing at all about this "world" business, but thank him with all my heart that he is my Redeemer.

At risk of monotony let me say again: the character of the world is morally different from the Spirit-imparted life we have received from God. Fundamentally it is because we possess this new life of God's gift that the world hates us, for it has no hatred for its own kind. This radical difference leaves us indeed with no way of making the world love us. "If ye were of the world, the world would love its own: but because ye are not of the world, but I chose you out of the world, therefore the world hateth you."

When the world meets in us a natural human honesty and decency, it appreciates this, and is ready to pay us due respect and place in us its confidence. But as soon as it meets that in us which is not of ourselves, namely the divine nature of which we have been made partakers, its hostility is at once aroused. Show the world the fruits of Christianity and it will applaud; show it Christianity and it will oppose it vigorously. For let the world evolve as it will, it can never produce one Christian. It can imitate Christian honesty, Christian courtesy, Christian charity, yes, but to produce one single Christian it can never aspire. A so-called Christian civilization gains the recognition and respect of the world. The world can tolerate that; it can even assimilate and utilize that. But Christian life— the life of Christ in the Christian believer: that it hates, and wherever it meets it it will assuredly oppose it to the death.

Christian civilization is the outcome of an attempt to reconcile the world and Christ. In Old Testament figure we see that represented by Moab and Ammon, the fruit indirectly of Lot's involvement and compromise with Sodom; and neither Moab nor Ammon proved any less hostile to Israel than were the heathen nations. Christian civilization proves that it can mix with the world, and may even be found taking the world's side in a crisis. There is one thing, however, that is eternally apart from the world and can never mix with it, and that is the life of Christ. Their natures are mutually antagonistic and cannot be reconciled. Between the finest specimen of human nature the world can produce and the most insignificant Christian there is no common ground, and thus no basis of comparison. For natural goodness is something we had by natural birth and can by our own resources naturally develop; but spiritual goodness is, in John's words, "begotten of God" (1 John 5:4).

God has established in the world a universal Church; and in one place and another he has planted many local churches. God, I say, has done this. It would be unreasonable therefore to expect that his way of deliverance from the world would be by physical separation from it. But as a consequence many sincere Christians are greatly perplexed by the problem of absorption. If God plants a local church here, will it, they ask, one day be reabsorbed by the world?

That in fact presents no problem to the living God. Inasmuch as its origin is not of the world, there is in the family of God no correspondence whatever with the world and thus no possibility of the world absorbing it. This is of course no credit to us, his children. It is not because we earnestly desire to be heavenly that the Church is heavenly, but because we are born out of heaven. And if, by our heavenly origin, we are absolved from trying to work our way there, we are absolved also thereby from studying to keep ourselves physically clear of this world.

How can the world possibly mix with what is otherworldly? For all that is of the world is empty dust, whereas all that is of God has the miraculous quality of divine life. Some of our brothers in Nanking were once assisting in relief work after the bombing of the city by Japanese planes. Suddenly, as they stood before a shattered house wondering where to begin, there was a violent upheaval of bricks and timbers, and a man emerged. Shaking the dust and rubble from him he rose and struggled to his feet. The fallen beams and rafters fell back into place behind him and the dust settled again, but out he walked alive! While there is life what fear is there of mixture?

The prayer of Jesus to his Father which John records in Chapter 17 contains a plea that is most arresting. Having repeated the statement that "the world hated them, because they are not of the world, even as I am not of the world," Jesus continues: "I pray not that thou shouldest take them from (ek) the world, but that thou shouldest keep them from (ek) the evil one" (verses 14, 15).

Here we have an important principle which will occupy our next chapter. Christians have a vital place in the world. Though saved from the evil one and his system they have not yet been removed from his territory. They have a part to play there for which they are indispensable. Religious people, as we saw, attempt to overcome the world by getting out of it. As Christians, that is not our attitude at all. Right here is the place where we are called to overcome. Created distinct from the world, we accept with joy the fact that God has placed us in it. That distinctiveness, our gift from God in Christ, is all the safeguard we need.

6
Lights in the World

Without fear of challenge Jesus could say: "I am the light of the world" (John 8:12). His claim does not surprise us in the least. What *is* surprising, however, is that he should then say to his disciples, and so by implication to us: "Ye are the light of the world" (Matt. 5:14). For he does not exhort us to be that light; he plainly says that we *are* the world's light, whether we bring our illumination out into places where men can see it, or hide it away from them. The divine life planted in us, which itself is so utterly foreign to the world all around it, is a light source designed to illumine to mankind the world's true character by emphasizing through contrast its inherent darkness. Accordingly Jesus goes on: "Even so let your light shine before men, that they may see your good works, and glorify your Father which is in heaven." From this it is clear that to separate ourselves from the world today, and thus deprive it of its only light, in no way glorifies God. It merely thwarts his purpose in us and in mankind.

It is true that, as we saw earlier, the career of John the Baptist was rather different. He did in fact withdraw from the world to live austerely in desert places apart, subsisting, we are told, on locusts and wild honey. Men went out there to seek him, for even there he was a burning and a shining light. Yet we are reminded that "he was not that Light." He came only to bear witness to it. His testimony was the last and greatest of an old prophetic order, but it was so because it pointed forward to Jesus. Jesus alone was "the true Light which lighteth every man, coming into the world"; and he certainly "was in the world," not outside of it (John 1:9, 10). Christianity derives from him. God can use a John crying in the wilderness, but he never intended his Church to be a select company living by the principle of abstinence.

Earlier we saw how abstinence—"handle not, nor taste, nor touch"—was merely one more element in the world system, and as such was itself suspect (Col. 2:21). But we must go a stage further than this, and once again the apostle Paul comes to our help. In Romans 14:17 he shows how the Christian life is something removed altogether from controversy about what we do and what we don't do. "The kingdom of God is not eating and drinking"—not, that is to say, to be conceived in those terms at all—"but righteousness and peace and joy in the Holy Ghost," which are in a realm wholly different. The Christian lives, and is guided, not by rules specifying just how far he may mix with men, but by these inward qualities which are mediated to him by God's Holy Spirit.

Righteousness and peace and joy in the Holy Ghost: It may be good for a moment to direct our attention to the second of these. For peace, we find, is a potent element in God's answer to his Son's prayer that he would keep us from the evil one (John 17:15).

In God himself there is a peace, a profound undisturbedness of spirit, which keeps him untroubled and undistressed in the face of unspeakable conflict and contradiction. "In the world ye have tribulation," Jesus says, but "in me ye may have peace" (John 16:33). How easily we get troubled as soon as something goes wrong! But do we ever pause to consider what went wrong with the great purpose upon which God had set his heart? God, who is light, had an eternal plan. Causing light to shine out of darkness he designed this world to be the arena of that plan. Then Satan, as we know, stepped in to thwart God, so that men came to love darkness rather than light. Yet in spite of that setback, the implications of which we appreciate all too little, God preserves in himself a quite undisturbed peace. It is that peace of God which, Paul tells us, is to garrison our hearts and thoughts in Christ Jesus (Phil. 4:7).

What does "garrison" really mean? It means that my foe has to fight through the armed guard at the gates before he can reach me. Before I can be touched, the garrison itself has first to be overcome. So I dare to be as peaceful as God, for the peace that is keeping God is keeping me. This is something that the world knows nothing about. "Peace I leave with you; my peace I give unto you: not as the world giveth, give I unto you" (John 14:27).

How utterly men failed to understand Jesus! Whatever he did was wrong in their eyes, for the light that was in them was darkness. They even dared to identify the Spirit that was in him with Beelzebub the prince of devils. Yet when they accused him of gluttony and drunkenness, what was his response? "Father, I thank thee!" (Matt. 11:19, 25). He was unmoved, because in Spirit he abode in the peace of God.

Or recall that last night before his passion. Everything seemed to be going wrong: a friend going out into the night to betray him, another drawing a sword in anger, people going into hiding, or running away naked in their eagerness to escape. In the midst of it all Jesus said to those who had come to take him, "I am he," so peacefully and so quietly that instead of him being nervous it was they who trembled and fell backwards. This was an experience that has been repeated in the martyrs of every age. They could be

tortured or burned, but because they possessed
his peace, the onlookers could only wonder at
their dignity and composure. It is no surprise to
us therefore that Paul describes this peace as beyond understanding.

How striking is the contrast Jesus draws between "in the world" where we are to have tribulation, and "in me" where we may have peace. If
God has placed us in the one, to be thronged by
its pressures and claims and needs, he has
placed us also in the Other, to be held by him
undisturbed amid it all. Jesus himself once
asked, "Who touched me?" The believing touch
of one in that Capernaum multitude registered
with him. It matched his own heart of compassion, whereas the pressure of the rest crowding
upon him had no such effect. All their impatient
jostling did not touch him in the least, for there
was little in common between them and him.
"Not as the world giveth, give I unto you." If our
life is the life of men, we are swayed by the
world. If it is the life of the Spirit it is unmoved
by worldly pressures.

"Righteousness and peace and joy": with such
things is the kingdom of God concerned. Never
let us be drawn away, therefore, into the old
realm of "eating and drinking," for it is neither
the prescription of these things nor their prohibi-
tion that concerns us, but another world altogether. So we who are of the kingdom need not
abstain. We overcome the world not by giving up
the world's things but by being otherworldly in a
positive way: by possessing, that is, a love and a
joy and a peace that the world cannot give and

that men sorely need.

Far from seeking to avoid the world we need to see how privileged we are to have been placed there by God. "As thou didst send me into the world, even so send I them into the world." What a statement! The Church is Jesus' successor, a divine settlement planted here right in the midst of Satan's territory. It is something that Satan cannot abide, any more than he could abide Jesus himself, and yet it is something that he cannot by any means rid himself of. It is a colony of heaven, an alien intrusion on his territory, and one against which he is utterly powerless. "Children of God," Paul calls us, "in the midst of a crooked and perverse generation, among whom ye are seen as lights in the world" (Phil. 2:15). God has deliberately placed us in the *kosmos* to show it up for what it is. We are to expose to the divine light, for all men to see them, its God-defying rebelliousness on the one hand and its hollowness and emptiness on the other.

And our task does not stop there. We are to proclaim to men the good news that, if they will turn to it, that light of God in the face of Jesus Christ will set them free from the world's vain emptiness into the fullness that is his. It is this twofold mission of the Church that accounts for Satan's hatred. There is nothing that goads him so much as the Church's presence in the world. Nothing would please him more than to see its telltale light removed. The Church is a thorn in the side of God's adversary, a constant source of irritation and annoyance to him. We make a heap of trouble for Satan simply by *being* in the world. So why leave it?

"Go ye into all the world and preach the gospel" (Mark 16:15). This is the Christian's privilege. It is also his duty. Those who try to opt out of the world only demonstrate that they are still in some degree in bondage to its ways of thinking. We who are "not of it" have no reason at all to try to leave it, for *it is where we should be*.

So there is no need for us to give up our secular employments. Far from it, for they are our mission field. In this matter there are no secular considerations, only spiritual ones. We do not live our lives in separate compartments, as Christians in the Church and as secular beings the rest of the time. There is not a thing in our profession or in our employment that God intends should be dissociated from our life as his children. Everything we do, be it in field or highway, in shop, factory, kitchen, hospital or school, has spiritual value in terms of the kingdom of Christ. Everything is to be claimed for him. Satan would much prefer to have no Christians in any of these places, for they are decidedly in his way there. He tries therefore to frighten us out of the world, and if he cannot do that, to get us involved in his world system, thinking in its terms, regulating our behavior by its standards. Either would be a triumph for him. But for us to be in the world, yet with all our hopes, all our interests and all our prospects out of the world, that is Satan's defeat and God's glory.

Of Jesus' presence in the world it is written that "the darkness overcame it not" (John 1:5 margin). Nowhere in Scripture does it tell us of sin that we are to "overcome" it, but it distinctly says we are to overcome the world. In relation to sin God's word speaks only of deliverance; it is in relation to the world that it speaks of victory.

We need deliverance from sin, because God never intended we should have any touch with it; but we do not need, nor should we seek, deliverance from the world, for it is in the purpose of God that we touch it. We are not delivered out of the world, but being born from above, we have victory over it. And we have that victory in the same sense, and with the same unfailing certainty, that light overcame darkness.

"This is the victory that hath overcome the world, even our faith. And who is he that overcometh the world, but he that believeth that Jesus is the Son of God?" (1 John 5:4, 5). The key to victory is always our faith relationship with the victorious Son. "Be of good cheer," he said. "I have overcome the world" (John 16:33). Only Jesus could make such a claim; and he could do so because he could earlier affirm: "The prince of the world ... hath nothing in me" (John 14:30). It was the first time that anyone on earth had said such a thing. He said it, and he overcame. And through his overcoming the prince of the world was cast out and Jesus began to draw men to himself.

And because he said it, we now dare say it too. Because of my new birth, because "whatsoever is begotten of God overcometh the world," I can be in the same world as my Lord was in, and in the same sense as he was I can be utterly apart from it, a lamp set on a lampstand, giving light to all who enter the house. "As he is, so are we in this world" (1 John 4:17). The Church glorifies God, not by getting out of the world but by radiating his light in it. Heaven is not the place to glorify God; it will be the place to praise him. The place to glorify him is here.

7
Detachment

We have seen the Church as a thorn in Satan's side, causing him acute discomfort and reducing his freedom of movement. Though in the world, the Church not only refuses to aid in the world's construction but persists in pronouncing judgment upon it. But if this is true, if the Church is always a source of irritation to the world, then equally the world is a source of constant grief to the Church. And because the world is always developing, its power to distress God's people is ever expanding; in fact the Church has to meet a

force in the world today with which in the early
days she was not confronted at all. Then the
children of God met open persecution in the
shape of outward physical assault upon their
persons (Acts 12; 2 Corinthians 11). They were
always coming into collision with material, tangible things. Now the chief trouble they meet in
the world is more subtle, an intangible force behind its material things, that is not holy but spir-
itually evil. The impact of that spiritual force
today is far greater than it was then. And not
only is it greater; there is an element present now
that was not there formerly.

In Revelation 9 we read of a development
which, to the author of that book, lay far in the
future. "The fifth angel sounded, and I saw a star
from heaven fallen unto the earth: and there was
given to him the key of the pit of the abyss. And
he opened the pit of the abyss; and there went up
a smoke out of the pit, as the smoke of a great
furnace.... And out of the smoke came forth locusts upon the earth; and power was given them,
as the scorpions of the earth have power. And it
was said unto them that they should not hurt the
grass of the earth, neither any green thing,
neither any tree, but only such men as have not
the seal of God on their foreheads" (verses 1-4).
This is figurative language, but the star falling
from heaven obviously refers to Satan, and we
know that the bottomless pit is his domain—
his storehouse, we might say. Thus it appears
that the end time is to be marked by a special
release of his forces, and men will find themselves up against a spiritual power with which

they had not before to contend.

Surely this accords with conditions in our day. While it is true that sin and violence will be greater than ever at the close of this age, it is apparent from God's Word that it is not specifically these with which the Church will have to grapple then, but with the spiritual appeal of far more everyday things. "As it came to pass in the days of Noah, even so shall it be also in the days of the Son of man. They ate, they drank, they married, they were given in marriage, until the day that Noah entered into the ark, and the flood came and destroyed them all. Likewise even as it came to pass in the days of Lot; they ate, they drank, they bought, they sold, they planted, they builded; but in the day that Lot went out from Sodom it rained fire and brimstone from heaven, and destroyed them all" (Luke 17:26-29). The point being made here by Jesus is not that these things—food, marriage, trade, agriculture, engineering—were outstanding characteristics of Lot's and Noah's day, but that they will in a special way characterize the last days. "After the same manner shall it be in the day that the Son of man is revealed" (verse 30): that is the point. For these things are not inherently sinful; they are simply things of the world. Have you ever in all your days paid such attention to the good life as now? Food and raiment are becoming the special burden of God's children today. What shall we eat? What shall we drink? Wherewithal shall we be clothed? For many these are almost the sole topics of conversation. There is a power that forces you to consider these matters; your very existence demands that you pay attention to them.

And yet Scripture warns us that "the kingdom of God is not eating and drinking, but righteousness" and so on. It bids us first of all seek the kingdom of God and his righteousness, and assures us that as we do so, all these things will be added to us. It bids us be carefree regarding matters of food and clothing, for if God cares for the flowers of the field and the birds of the air, will he not much rather care for us, his own? Yet to judge by our anxieties it would almost seem that they are cared for, but not we!

Now here is the point that needs special emphasis. This condition of things is abnormal. The undue attention to eating and drinking, whether at the extremes of subsistence or luxury, that characterizes so many Christians these days is far from normal; it is supernatural. For it is not just a question of food and drink that we are meeting here; we are meeting demons. Satan conceived and now controls the world order, and is prepared to use demonic power through the things of the world to lure us into it. The present state of affairs cannot be accounted for apart from this. Oh that the children of God might awaken to this fact! In past days God's saints met all sorts of difficulties; yet, in the midst of pressure, they could look up and trust God. In the pressures of today, however, they are so confused and bewildered that they seem unable to trust him. Oh, let us realize the Satanic origin of all this pressure and confusion!

The same is true in matrimonial affairs. Never

have we met so many problems in this field as today. There is confusion abroad as young people break with old traditions but lack the guidance of any new ones to replace them. This fact is not to be accounted for naturally, but supernaturally. Marrying and giving in marriage are wholesome and normal in any age, but today there is an element breaking into these things that is unnatural.

So it is with planting and building, and so too with buying and selling. All these things can be perfectly legitimate and beneficial, but today the power behind them presses upon men until they are bewildered and lose their balance. The evil force that energizes the world system has pre-cipitated a condition today where we see two extremes; the one extreme of utter inability to make ends meet, and the other extreme of un-usual opportunity to amass wealth. On the one hand many Christians find themselves in un-precedented economic difficulties: on the other hand many are faced with no less unprecedented opportunities of enriching themselves. Both of these conditions are abnormal.

Enter any home these days and listen in on the conversation. You will hear remarks such as these: "Last week I bought such-and-such goods at such-and-such a figure, and I have thereby saved so much." "Happily I purchased that a year ago, otherwise I would have lost badly." "If you want to sell, sell now while the market is good." Have you not noticed the way people are rushing here and there, feverishly making busi-ness deals? Doctors are stocking up with flour, cloth manufacturers are selling paper, men and women who have never touched such things before are being swept off their feet by the current of speculation. They are caught up in a marketing maelstrom that is whirling them madly around. Do you not realize that this state of affairs is not natural? Do you not see that there is a power here which is captivating men? People are not acting sanely; they are beside themselves. Today's buying and selling spree is not just a question of making a little money—or losing it. It is a question of touching a Satanic system. We are living in the end time, a time when a special power has been let loose which is driving men on, whether they will or no.

So the question today is not so much one of sinfulness as of worldliness. Who would dare to say you do wrong to eat and drink? Who would dare to disapprove of marrying and giving in marriage? Who would question your right to buy and sell? These things are not in themselves wrong; the wrong lies in the spiritual force behind them, which, through their medium, presses relentlessly upon us. Oh that we might awake to the fact that, whereas these things are so common and so simple, they are yet being used by Satan to ensnare God's children into the great net of his world order.

"Take heed to yourselves, lest haply your hearts be overcharged with surfeiting, and drunkenness, and cares of this life, and that day come on you suddenly as a snare" (Luke 21:34). Note the term "life" in Jesus' words. In the Greek New Testament three words are commonly used for life: *zoe*, spiritual life; *psuche*, psychological life; and *bios*, biological life. The last is the word used here, appearing in its adjectival form, *biotikos*, "of this life." The Lord is warning us to beware lest we be unduly pressed with this life's cares, that is to say, with anxieties regarding quite ordinary matters such as food and dress which belong to our present existence on the earth. It was over just such a simple thing that Adam and Eve fell, and it will be due to just such simple matters that some Christians may overlook the heavenward call of God. For it is always a matter of where the heart is. We are exhorted not to let our hearts be "overcharged" or "laden" with these things to our loss. That is to say, we are not to carry a burden regarding them that would weigh us down. We are to be in a true sense detached in spirit from our goods in the house or in the field (Luke 17:31).

For let us realize who we are! We are the Church, the light of the world shining amid the darkness. As such let us live our lives down here.

There was a time when the Church rejected the world's ways. Now she not only uses them; she abuses them. Of course we must use the world, because we need it; but let us not want it, let us not desire it. So Jesus continues, "Watch ye at every season, making supplication, that ye may prevail to escape all these things that shall come to pass and to stand (literally 'be set') before the Son of man" (Luke 21:36). Would God urge us to watch and pray were there not a spiritual force to guard against? We dare not take our destiny as a

matter of course, but must be constantly on the
alert that we be truly disentangled in spirit from
the elements of this world. There are things of
the world that are essential to our very existence.
To be concerned with them is legitimate, but to
be weighed down by them is illegitimate and
may cause us to forfeit God's best.

The book of Revelation suggests that Satan
will set up his kingdom of antichrist in the political world (Ch. 13), in the religious world (Ch.
17), and in the commercial world (Ch. 18). On
this threefold basis of politics, religion and
commerce, his reign will find its last violent expression. In the latter two chapters this kingdom
appears under the figure of Babylon, the special
instrument of Satan. Babylon seems to represent
corrupted Christianity—Rome perhaps, but big-
ger and more insidious than Rome—and it is on
the ground of her commerce that she is judged.
The whole record of Chapter 18 revolves around
merchants and merchandise. Those who bemoan
the great city's fall, from the king right down to
the ships' helmsmen, all bewail the thought that
her flourishing trade has suddenly ceased. Evidently it is neither religion nor politics but trade
that causes the spirit of Babylon to flourish
again, and that is bewailed in her downfall. We
dare not emphatically state that pure commerce
is wrong, but this we do say on the ground of
God's own Word, that its beginning is connected
with Satan (Ezek. 28) and its end with Babylon
(Rev. 18). And this we add from hard earned experience, that commerce is the field in which,
more than in any other, "the corruption that is in

the world through lust" relentlessly pursues even the most high-principled of Christians, and apart from the grace of God, will all too easily overtake them to their undoing.

Are we sensitive to Babylon? The merchants wept, but heaven cried Hallelujah! (19:1). These (verses 1-6) are the only Hallelujahs recorded in the New Testament. Do we reecho them?

For we are in a perilous realm when we touch commerce. If by reason of our calling we engage in pure trade, and if we do so in fear and trembling, we may with God's help escape the snare of the Devil. But if we are overconfident, then there is no hope of escape from the unscrupulous self-seeking that such business engenders. So the problem that confronts us these days is not how to refrain from buying and selling, from eating and drinking, marrying and giving in marriage; the problem now is to avoid the power behind these things, for we dare not let that power triumph over us.

What, then, is the secret of holding our material things in the will of God? Surely it is to hold them *for God*, that is to say, to know we are not hoarding useless valuables, or amassing vast bank deposits, but laying up treasures to his account. You and I must be perfectly willing to part with anything at any moment. It matters not whether I leave two thousand dollars or merely two. What matters is whether I can leave whatever I have without a twinge of regret.

I am not suggesting by this that we must try to dispose of everything; that is not the point. The point is that as God's children you and I may not accumulate things for ourselves. If I keep something it is because God has spoken to my heart; if I part with it it is for the same reason. I hold *myself* in the will of God and am not afraid to give if God asks me to give. I keep nothing because I love it, but let it go without regret when the call comes to leave it behind. That is what it means to be detached, free, separated to God.

8
Mutual Refreshing

In John's Gospel there is recorded an event which only he has preserved for us. It is an event full of divine meaning and one which greatly helps to illumine for us this problem of living in the world. I refer to the incident in Chapter 13 in which our Lord Jesus girds himself with a towel, and taking a basin, washes his disciples' feet. This action of Jesus has lessons to teach us which I do not propose to go into fully here. Instead I want us to look in particular at his command which follows it. "Ye also ought to wash one another's feet. For I have given you an example, that ye should also do as I have done to you.... If ye know these things, blessed are ye if ye do them" (verses 14-17). What is this mutual feetwashing? What does it mean that I should wash my brother's feet and that my feet should be washed by my brother?

The aspect of truth specially emphasized here is refreshment. As we shall shortly see, it is something very dear to the Lord that we as his children should learn to minister refreshment to our brethren, and that they in turn should be a means of refreshment to our spirits.

Let me say at once that this passage does not concern sins. Whether I go barefoot or wearing sandals, or even shoes, the dust that gathers on my feet is something inevitable. I cannot avoid it. But for me to have a fall, and having fallen to roll in the dust so that it collects on my body and on my clothes—that is not inevitable; it is altogether wrong! I have to walk from one place to another, but it is quite unnecessary for me to roll along the street in order to get there. I can do so without floundering in the mud!

Equally in the Christian life, to stumble and fall and then to flounder in the dust is sin, certainly. It calls for repentance and it needs God's forgiveness. For it is not necessary for me to walk with the Lord like that, hiding behind the excuse that "I must fall once in a while; it is inevitable!" That, we all agree, is wrong.

But the point about the dust on our feet is this, that in walking through the world, no matter who we are or how careful we may be, it is inevitable that our feet will collect something. Of course if we do not touch the earth at all, we certainly pick up nothing, but to achieve this we should have to be carried around. If we do touch the ground—and who seriously expects not to?—we are certain to pick up what is there. Even our Lord Jesus rebuked his host with the words: "Thou gavest me no water for my feet" (Luke 7:44). So please remember that the mutual washing in John 13 is not concerned with sins committed, for which there is always forgiveness through the Blood, but from which anyway God intends that we should be delivered. No, it is concerned rather with our daily walk through the world, during which it is unavoidable that we shall contract something. "Ye are clean," Jesus says. The precious Blood sees to that. "He that is bathed needeth not ..." and as far as sin is concerned the sentence might end there. But move about in Satan's kingdom and something certainly clings to us. Like a film upon us it comes between us and our Lord. This is inescapable, simply because we are touching the world's things all the time, its business and its pleasures, its corrupt scale of values and its whole ungodly outlook. Hence the words with which Jesus concludes: "... save *to wash his feet*."

So let us come now to the practical outworking of this. Some of you brothers and sisters in Christ have to go out to work in offices or shops for, say, seven or eight hours a day. It is not wrong that you do so. It is not sin to work in a shop or a factory. But when you come home from your place of employment, do you not find your-

self tired and dispirited and out of tune with
things? You meet a brother, but you cannot slip
easily and directly into speaking with him of divine things. It is as though there were a coating
of something contaminating you. I repeat: that is
not necessarily sin at all; it is just that your contact with the world has deposited upon you that
film of tarnish. You cannot help feeling it, for
there seems to be an inability to rise up to the
Lord at once. The luminous touch which you
had with him in the morning seems to have been
darkened; its freshness has gone from you. We
all know that experience.

Or again, some of our sisters have to attend to
domestic duties. Let us suppose a young mother
is preparing dinner and has something cooking
on the stove. All at once the baby cries, the door
bell rings, the milk boils over—everything
comes upon her together in a rush. She runs to
one and misses the other! After everything is
eventually settled she sits down, and it seems as
if she needs a power to lift her up to God again.
She is conscious of something there—not sin,
but as it were a deposit of dust over everything. It
clings like a film, coming between her and her
Lord, and she feels tarnished, soiled. There is not
that clear way which takes her through to God at
once. This I think illustrates for us the need of
feetwashing.

Many a time we are tired and jaded by our
secular duties. When we get down to pray, we
find we have to wait for awhile. It seems to take
us ten or twenty minutes to come back to that
place where we can really get through to God. Or

if we sit down to read the Word, we find it requires a determined effort to restore again that openness to his speaking. But how good it is if on the road home we meet a brother with an overflowing heart, fresh from communion with God! Without meaning to do anything he just spontaneously shakes our hand and says, "Brother, praise the Lord!" He may not know it, but somehow it is as if he has come with a duster and wiped everything clean. Immediately we feel that our touch with God has been restored.

Sometimes you may come into a prayer meeting with a heavy spirit, through the effect of your work during the day. Someone may pray, and you still feel the same; and another prays, and there is no difference. But then another brother or sister prays, and somehow you immediately feel the lifting power. You are refreshed; your feet have been washed. What, then, does washing mean? It means to restore to the original freshness. It means to bring things back to a point of such clearness that it is once again as though they came out of God's immediate presence, new from his hand.

I do not know how many times I personally have felt low like that, when it was not exactly sin that was troubling, but that feeling of a coating of the world's dust; and then I have met a brother or a sister, one who may have known nothing at all of my condition, but who has just passed on a remark that has brightened everything. When this happens you simply feel all the darkness gone, the film swept away. Praise God, you are refreshed and put back at once into the condition where you can directly enjoy touch with him again. That is feetwashing—to refresh my brethren in Christ; to bring a brother again to the place where it is as though he had just come out from the very presence of God. It is this ministry to one another that the Lord desires to see among his children.

If we are walking with God there is not a day when we may not, if we wish, be a refreshment to our brethren. This is one of the greatest ministries. It may be no more than a handshake. It may be a word of encouragement almost casually spoken. It may be just the light of heaven on our faces. But if the Lord has got his way with us and we are in the state of having no cloud between ourselves and him, we shall find that we are quietly being used. We may not know it, for it is better not to seek to know it—indeed it may be better *never* to know it. But whether we know it or not, we are constantly being used to refresh our brother. When he is low and in darkness, when he has a burden on his heart or a film before his eyes, when he has been tarnished and stained, then to us he will come. He may not stay long, perhaps only for a few minutes. Seek for that ministry. Find grace from God to help him. Often we think it would be good if we could give long sermons that command a wide hearing, but few have that gift, and many are not reached by those few who have. To refresh the hearts of the saints is the kind of ministry which everyone can fulfill and which can reach everywhere. In the valuation of God it is without price.

But to serve others in this way we must fulfill

the conditions. If we are really going on with the Lord there is of course no question that we shall be used, for there are no limitations with him. If we ourselves are untarnished, with hearts brimming with his joy and peace, there is bound to be an overflow. So the simple question I put to you is this: Is there any point of controversy between you and God? I refer of course to real, known issues. If there is nothing special, then there is no need for you to search around to find something; the Lord himself will always discover it. When *he* wants to bring to light something you are overlooking, he will always point his finger there, and you will know it. There is no need for you to turn your eyes within and by checking up and analyzing every feeling to try to dig it out. Just praise him! It is the Lord's business, not yours, to shine into your heart and show you when you are astray from him.

But one thing is certain. If you do have a controversy with God, you can only tarnish others. You can never wash their feet. When they are low, you will bring them lower. When they feel heavy, you will come to them and make them heavier still. Instead of refreshing them and restoring to them the newness that comes out from God, you can only plunge them into deeper gloom. To be at odds with God is the sure way to be a drain upon the life of his Church, whereas the greatest manifestation of power is, I believe, to be able constantly to refresh others. It is a priceless thing, that touch of heaven that lifts, cleanses, renews.

"Ye also ought to wash one another's feet." Of

all his commandments to his disciples this is—and I use the expression in its purest sense—the most dramatic. To impress on them its importance he himself acted it out before them. It was an expression of his love for "his own which were in the world" (verse 1). He set himself to show his disciples what he meant by ministry. It is not platform work. It is serving one another with a basin and a towel. There will always be a need of restoring people who have fallen, of bringing back to repentance the weak ones who have sinned; but the greatest need of the saints today is of refreshment, by which I mean recalling them afresh to what is original and of God. That is power. Jesus himself "came forth from God" (verse 3) to do this. I do not know how it strikes you, but I think there is no greater power for God than to be fresh from him before the world. Do you not find it to be the greatest manifestation of the power of divine life? In a world system darkened with the smoke of the pit, how we rejoice to meet saints who are fresh with the clean air of heaven. Such freshness brings anew to you and me the divine breath of life.

I thank the Lord that in my younger days I had the great privilege of knowing one of the rarest of saints. I knew her for many years, and found her to have many spiritual qualities; but I think the thing that impressed me above them all was the sense of God. You could not for long sit in her presence, or even walk into her room and have a handshake, without feeling a sense of God coming over you. You did not know why, but you felt it. I was not the only one who felt this. Everyone who had touch with her gave the same testimony. I have to confess that in those days many a time I was feeling downhearted, and it seemed as though everything had gone wrong. I walked into her room, and immediately I felt rebuked. Immediately I felt I was face to face with God, I was refreshed.

Why should this thing happen, this immediate restoration? Surely not because it is just the ministry of a privileged few. The Lord would like every single one of us to be like that, to impart that power to brighten our brothers and sisters when they have become tarnished. Please remember—dare I say this?—that sometimes being tarnished does more to hurt the impact of the Christian's life upon the world than do his actual, conscious sins. Once in a while we may sin, any of us, but because we are sensitive to that, we know at once that we have done so and will seek and find forgiveness. But many a time we have been tarnished for hours with the world's tarnish, and because it is not actual sin we remain unconcerned. Then it is that our impact for God upon the world becomes blunted. How good it is at such a time to have around a brother or sister through whom we are lifted once more to a renewed communion with God!

What, then, are the rules? They are two. First, as we have seen, there must be no known discord between me and my Lord that is not at once cleared up; for if there is, that effectively puts me out of this ministry altogether. Whatever the matter be, it is to be settled at once or I am use-

less. Far from being an asset to the Church of
God I have become only a burden. I can contribute nothing; I can only add to the debit side of
the life of his children. In order to be a con-
tributor, there must be a transparent clearness
between me and God on every conscious issue.
Then, free of such disharmony, I too may be the
means of lifting my brethren back to their place
of power against the world.

Secondly—and to avoid misunderstanding
this needs stating plainly: please remember that
this refreshing is mutual. "Wash one another's
feet," Jesus said. The refresher must expect also
to be refreshed by others. Many a time the Lord
may use you, but equally, many a time he may
use someone else to refresh you. There exist no
chosen few set apart for a spiritual task as "re-
freshers," just as none of us are absolved from
walking through this world and needing therefore to be refreshed. As with Peter, no single one
of us is entitled to say of himself: "I have gone
beyond that stage. I am now in such touch with
God that I am above tarnish, and can pray or
preach without the need of such a ministry.
Thou shalt never wash my feet!"

No superior class of brothers exists in the
Church that has no need to be refreshed. It is
something every servant of God depends on.
Employed in a workshop or a kitchen all day,
you may well need brightening up; but some of
us have been working all day in churches, and
we too need to be brightened! Our need of restoration is often just as great, though we may well
be lulled into overlooking that fact. Whether we

work in any obviously secular sphere or are engaged in so-called spiritual things, the world is all around us, closing in. Ever and anon therefore we need the help of some brother or sister to lift us again to that fresh touch of God, that renewal of divine power.

Thus the principle of the Body is, quite simply, refreshing and being refreshed. The more we go on with the Lord the more we need the brethren. For in this ministry not one of us is insignificant, and not one of us ever reaches the point where he has no need to be ministered to by another. My prayer for myself is that God may once in a while use me to refresh someone else's spirit when it is jaded, and that likewise he may once in a while use someone else to touch my flagging spirit and refresh me. If by that brother the tarnish of the world is wiped off me, so that coming weary I go away renewed, then his has been a ministry of Christ to me.

What I have thus sought to describe in simple terms amounts to a united front against the world. This is no small thing. If we will believe it enough to practice it, it possesses, I am convinced, the power to make Satan's mightiest strongholds tremble. In Jesus' words: "If ye know these things, blessed are ye if ye do them."

9
My Laws in Their Hearts

In earlier chapters we have been building up a picture of this world, not just as a location, nor as a race of people, nor indeed as anything merely material, but rather as a spiritual system at the head of which is God's enemy. "The world" is Satan's masterpiece, and we have thought of him as directing all his strength and ingenuity into causing it to flourish. To what end? Surely to capture men's allegiance and draw them to himself. He has one object: to establish his own dominion in human hearts worldwide. Even though he must be aware that that dominion may last only briefly, that, without question, is his goal. And as the end of the age approaches and his efforts increase, so does the distress of God's people intensify. For as aliens and sojourners, their position—in the world and yet not of it—is an uncomfortable one. They would fain seek relief from the spiritual tension in physical distance. How good it would be to escape from this world completely and be forever with the Lord!

But clearly that is not his will. As we saw, he prayed the Father not to take his own out of the world but to preserve them there from the evil one. And Paul takes a similar line. Having in a particular instance exhorted the Corinthian believers not to have fellowship with a certain class of sinner, he immediately takes steps to guard against possible misunderstanding. They are not to isolate themselves. They are not to sever connections with all sinners in the world, nor even with those in the category described, for to do so would involve their leaving the world altogether. "I wrote unto you in my epistle to have no company with fornicators; not altogether (i.e. not at all meaning) with the fornicators of this world, or with the covetous and extortioners, or with idolators; for then must ye needs go out of the world" (1 Cor. 5:9, 10).

It is clear from Paul's words therefore that we may, and indeed must, associate with the world to a certain extent, for is it not the world that God so loved? But here is the question: To what extent? How far may we go? All of us agree that we are obliged at some points to touch the things of the world. But presumably there is a limit somewhere. Keep within that limit and we are safe; exceed it and we risk becoming implicated by Satan.

I do not think we can exaggerate this problem, for it is an acute one and the dangers are real. If the time should come when you are acutely ill and in great pain, and the doctor should prescribe for you heroin or morphine, you would instantly be alive to the danger of developing a craving for the drug. You would obey him and take the treatment, but you would take it fearfully and prayerfully, for you know there is a power in it, and you know you are liable to come under that power. This would be especially so if the treatment had to be prolonged.

Every time you and I touch the world through the things of the world—and we must do so repeatedly—we should feel much as we would feel about taking morphine, for there are demons at the back of everything that belongs to the world. Just as I may, if seriously ill, be prescribed opium as a treatment, so also, because I am still in the world, I have to do business with the world, follow some trade or employment, earn my livelihood. But how much treatment with dangerous drugs I can safely take without falling a prey to the opium craving I do not know; and how many things I can buy, or how much money I can make, or how close can be my business or professional associations, without my becoming hooked, I likewise do not know. All I know is that there is a Satanic power behind every worldly thing. How vital therefore for every

Christian to have a clear revelation of the spirit of the world in order to appreciate how real is the danger to which he is continually exposed!

Perhaps you think I am going too far. Perhaps you say: Oh yes, that may be a good sermon illustration, but I find it hard not to feel you are overstating the case. But when you *see*, then you will say of the world, as you say of opium, that there is a sinister power behind it, a power designed to seduce and to captivate men. Those whose eyes have been really opened to this world's true character find they must touch everything in it with fear and trembling, looking continually to the Lord. They know that at any moment they are liable to be caught in Satan's entanglements. Just as the drug which, in the first instance, is welcomed to relieve sickness may ultimately become itself a cause of sickness, so equally the things of the world which we can legitimately use under the Lord's authority may, if we are heedless, become a cause of our downfall. Only fools can be careless in circumstances like these.

No wonder we look with envy upon John the Baptist! How easy, we feel, if like him we could simply withdraw into a safe place apart! But we are *not* like him. Our Lord has sent us into the world in his own footsteps, "both eating and drinking." Since God so loved, his command to us is to go "into all the world" and proclaim his good news; and surely that "all" includes the folk with whom we must rub shoulders daily!

So a serious problem faces us here. As we have said, presumably there must be a limit. Presumably God has drawn somewhere a line of demar-

cation. Stay within the bounds of that line and
we will be safe; cross it and grave danger
threatens. But where does it lie? We have to eat
and drink, to marry and bring up children, to
trade and to toil. How do we do so and yet remain uncontaminated? How do we mingle freely
with the men and women whom God so loved as
to give his Son for them, and still keep ourselves
unspotted from the world?

If our Lord had limited our buying and selling
to so much a month, how simple that would be!
The rules would be plain for any to follow. All
who spent more than a certain amount per
month would be worldly Christians, and all who
spent less than that amount would be unworldly.

But since our Lord has stipulated no figure, we
are cast on him unceasingly. For what? I think
the answer is very wonderful. Not to be tied by
the rules, but that we may remain all the time
within bounds of another kind: the bounds of his
life. If our Lord had given us a set of rules and
regulations to observe, then we could take great
care to abide by these. In fact however our task is
something far more simple and straightforward,
namely, to abide in the Lord himself. Then we
could keep the law. Now we need only keep in
fellowship with him. And the joy of it is that,
provided we live in close touch with God, his
Holy Spirit within our hearts will always tell us
when we reach the limit!

We spoke earlier of the kingdom of antichrist,
soon to be revealed. John, in his epistle, writing
to his "little children" about the world and the
things of the world (1 John 2:15) goes on to warn

them: "As ye heard that antichrist cometh, even now have there arisen many antichrists" (verse 18). Faced with these, and with that even more insidious "spirit of the antichrist, whereof ye have heard that it cometh; and now it is in the world already" (4:3), what are they to do? How are they in their simplicity to know what is true and what is false? How are they possibly to tell which ground is treacherous to walk upon and which is safe?

The answer John gives them is so simple that today we are afraid to believe it. "Ye have an anointing from the Holy One, and ye know all things.... The anointing which ye received of him abideth in you, and ye need not that anyone teach you: but as his anointing teacheth you concerning all things, and is true, and is no lie, and even as it taught you, ye abide in him" (2:20, 27). This is certainly an allusion to the Spirit of truth, who, Jesus promised his disciples, would both convict the world and guide them into all the truth (John 16:8-13).

In any given instance there must be safe limits known to God beyond which we should not go. They are not marked out on the ground for us to see, but one thing is certain: He who is the Comforter will surely know them, even if perhaps Satan knows them too. Can we not trust him? If at some point we are about to overstep them, can we not depend on him at once to make us inwardly aware of the fact?

In 1 Corinthians 7 the apostle Paul offers us some further guidance on the same theme. "This I say, brethren, the time is shortened, that hence-

forth both those that have wives may be as
though they had none; and those that weep, as
though they wept not; and those that rejoice, as
though they rejoiced not; and those that buy, as
though they possessed not; and those that use
the world, as not abusing it; for the fashion of
this world passeth away. I would have you to be
free from cares" (verses 29-32). Here several matters are in turn touched upon, but the governing
factor in them all is clearly this, that "the time is
shortened," or, as some translators render it,
"straitened." We are living, the apostle says, in
days of peculiar pressure, and the principle that
must guide us for such days is this, "that they
who have ... be as not having."

Does Paul, we wonder, contradict himself? In
Ephesians 5 he enjoins husbands to love their
wives with as perfect a love as that with which
Christ loved the Church—no less. Yet here he
tells them to live as though not having wives at
all! Does he honestly, we exclaim in dismay, expect us at one and the same time to reconcile
such complete opposites?

Here at once it must be said that such a
paradoxical life is a life that none but Christians
can live. Perhaps the expression "as not having"
affords us a clue. It reveals that the matter is an
inner matter, a question of the heart's loyalty. In
Christ there is an inner liberation to God, not
merely an outward change of conduct. They
have, and having, they rejoice in Ephesians 5;
but they are not bound by what they possess, so
that having not, they equally rejoice in 1 Corinthians 7. Notwithstanding all they "have," they

are so truly delivered in spirit from the world's possessiveness that they can live "as not having."

The natural man lives at one extreme or the other—either having, and being wholly taken up with what he has, or if he is religious, putting away what he has so that he no longer has it, and so being no longer concerned with it at all. But the Christian way is utterly different from the natural way. The Christian way to solve the problem is not by removing the thing, but by delivering the heart from the grip of that thing. The wife is not removed, nor the affection for the wife, but both wife and husband are freed from the overweening dominance of that affection. So, too, the trouble that caused weeping is not removed, but the life is no longer controlled by that trouble. The cause of joy still remains, but there is an inner check against vain abandon to the thing that caused it. Buying and selling go on as before, but an inward deliverance has loosened the personal grip upon them. We have them all, but we have them "as not having."

We talk sometimes about our desire to maintain, like John, the testimony of Jesus in the earth. Let us remember that that testimony is based, not on what *we* can say about this or that, but on what Satan can say *about us*. God has put us in the world, and often he locates us in some specially difficult places, where we are tempted to feel that worldlings have a much easier time than do Christians. That is because Christians are indeed aliens, living here in an element that is not naturally theirs. A swimmer may dive deep into the sea, but without special clothing and an airline to the atmosphere that is his own, he cannot stay there. The pressure is too great and he must breathe the air of the world to which he belongs. He stays deep as long as there is a task to do and as long as he is supplied with the power to overcome the element around him, but he does not belong to the element and *it has no part in him.*

Thus it is that the problem of our touch with the world is not solved by any change of outward action. Some think that, at a time like this in which we are living, it is a sign of spirituality to make no provision for the coming days. That is not spirituality, it is folly. What we may *do* with the provision we make is a question we shall consider in our final chapter, but God's word makes it plain that we are to use the world. We are to eat and drink, to trade merchandise and grow crops, to rejoice, yes and if need be to weep, and yet not to use any of these things to the full. We have learned what is at stake in all our relationships with the world. It is no wonder therefore that we have learned also to tread softly, heedful all the while of the Comforter's gentle constraining.

Jesus came "from above." He could claim without fear of challenge: "The prince of this world cometh and hath nothing in me." The line of demarcation was drawn, not on the ground at his feet but in his own heart. But just as truly, everything in this world that is "from above" is as safe as he is. God is at the head of the airline working the pumps, as it were. A life that be-

longs above is being sustained and provided for
down here *by him*. Thus it comes about that if a
thing is spiritual and "of God," we need not
worry about it nor contend for its preservation.
"My kingdom is not of this world, else would my
servants fight." They have no need to.

God does not worry about us, simply because
he has no anxiety about his Holy Spirit. There is
a sense in which poor quality spiritual life is
impossible, because spiritual life is God's life;
and just as truly, spiritual life can only be overwhelmed if God himself can be overwhelmed.
God does not argue about this fact. He is content
to leave it to the Comforter to make it real in us.
"Ye are of God, my little children, and have
overcome them; because greater is he that is in
you than he that is in the world" (1 John 4:4).

Again, the same verse which tells us that the
whole world lies in the lap of the evil one—yes,
the very same verse!—assures us once more that
"we are of God" (1 John 5:19). *We are of God!*
Could we possibly discover a more blessed fact
to balance against that other ugly fact and to
outweigh it? We who believe on Jesus' name
"were born, not of blood, nor of the will of the
flesh, nor of the will of man, but of God" (John
1:13). And praise him, because we are begotten
of God, the evil one cannot touch us (1 John
5:18).

Put very simply, Satan's power in the world is
everywhere. Yet wherever men and women walk
in the Spirit, sensitive to the anointing they have
from God, that power of his just evaporates.
There *is* a line drawn by God, a boundary where

by virtue of his own very presence Satan's writ does not run. Let God but occupy all the space himself, and what room is left for the evil one?

Are we thus utterly for God? Can Satan testify of you and me: "I cannot entrap that man!"?

10
The Powers of the Age to Come

What does the writer to the Hebrews mean when he says of Christians that they have "tasted ... the powers of the age to come" (Heb. 6:5)? We would all readily agree that there is a splendid future age to which we look forward. In it the kingdom that is now "in the midst" of us in terms of the mighty acts of the Spirit of God (Matt. 12:28) will then become universally visible and unchallenged. The kingdom of the world will have become the kingdom of our God and of his Christ (Rev. 11:15). But what, we may wonder, are these "powers" that now we only taste but cannot as yet feast upon? Clearly they are to be received and enjoyed, for the word "taste" implies not merely a doctrine to be thought about and analyzed, but something subjectively experienced and made our own. These powers are the preliminaries of a feast of which there is much more to follow but of which we already eat just a little.

We could list a number of such things to which Scripture looks forward. There is a salvation to be revealed in the last time (1 Pet. 1:5). There is a fresh aspect of eternal life in the age to come (Luke 18:30). There is a rest remaining to the people of God (Heb. 4:9). There will be the raising and renewal of our mortal bodies (Rom. 8:23; 1 Cor. 15:14). There will be a day when everything that stumbles men will be removed (Jer. 31:9; Isa. 57:14; 62:10). There will be a time when all shall know the Lord from the least to the greatest (Jer. 31:34; Heb. 8:11) and indeed when the earth shall be filled with the knowledge of the glory of the Lord as the waters cover the sea (Isa. 11:9; Hab. 2:14). Of all these things we have now a real foretaste in Christ, but we do not yet see them in completeness.

More directly related to our present study are the following considerations. The Epistle to the Hebrews applies to our Lord Jesus the words from Psalm 8: "Thou didst put all things in subjection under his feet," and then goes on quite frankly to express what experience generally must compel us to admit, namely, that "we see not yet all things subjected to him" (Heb. 2:8).

But alongside these two contrasting statements we must place also that of Jesus in Luke 10:19, where he already gives to his disciples "authority ... over all the power of the enemy." Surely this promises to us a *present* foretaste of that future day that we do not yet see.

Again, in the same Gospel passage, Jesus is recorded as saying, "I beheld Satan fallen as lightning from heaven" (10:18). This event John, in Revelation 12:9, seems to place far in the future. Yet clearly Jesus implies that from the standpoint of the witnessing Church it is already in some sense a present fact. Furthermore, in a later chapter of Revelation John is shown a day when Satan is to be bound with a chain for a thousand years (20:1-4). Yet Jesus speaks of "the strong man" as already bound, so that we may even now break into his house and despoil it (Matt. 12:29).

These are significant statements; for surely if we possess salvation and eternal life in the present, as we most certainly do, then we should also be knowing some foretastes today of the rest of these future "powers." For though not yet manifest universally, they are quite evidently fruits of the Cross and resurrection of Christ that must be, at least in principle, the Church's present possession.

God's eternal purpose is bound up with man. "Let us make man in our image, after our likeness," he said, "and let them have dominion." God intended man to wield power, to reign and rule, to control other created things. We cannot say that redemption was God's design—or even a

part of it—for man was never intended to fall,
still less to perish. Genesis 3 represents man's
history, not God's purpose for him. A workman
may fall from the fifth story of a building under
construction, but that was never in the ar-
chitect's plan!

No, God's plan is concerned with man's
dominion, and it is well to note the special
sphere of this, namely, "all the earth" (Gen.
1:26). Heaven has no problem; the problem is on
earth. Man is told to "subdue it" (verse 28) and
we ask ourselves why. If there were no forces to
be subdued, why this need? Furthermore we are
told that the Lord God took the man and put him
into the Garden of Eden to dress it and "to keep
it" (2:15). This is more than the usual Hebrew
word for "to keep." Adam is to guard God's
Paradise, and again this implies the proximity of
an enemy to be kept at bay.

It is interesting to note the wording of Genesis
1:26. Man is to have dominion "over all the
earth," and the clause is expanded to cover,
among other things, "every creeping thing that
creepeth upon the earth." But in the event the
first thing that man failed to control was a creeping thing, a worm. And by man's failure Satan
obtained, in a new way in man himself, legal
rights on the earth. True, the dust of the earth
was the lowly sphere appointed to him. "Upon
thy belly shalt thou go, and dust shalt thou eat"
(3:14). But what is dust? It is the substance of
which Adam was made! Thus man in the flesh is
now morally subject to Satan. God's foe has secured a clear title to all that by natural birth man

is and has. Natural human life is the foothold
here on earth of Satan's activity. Satan's world
springs from and finds its strength in his rights
in man, and even God does not dispute these
rights. He has acquired by Adam's default a full
title to all that is of the old creation.

If Satan is to cease to act in us, then his ground
in us must be taken from him. So God meets the
situation in redemption, not by dealing with
Satan directly but, as we have seen, by taking the
whole of the old creation—the man himself, his
world, everything—clean out of the way, and
thus removing from Satan his legal stand. Satan's overthrow is compassed not by a direct
blow aimed at him, but indirectly by the removal
from him in the death of Christ of all that gives
him the moral right of control. "Our old man was
crucified with him, that the body of sin might be
done away, so that we should no longer be in
bondage to sin" (Rom. 6:6).

Praise God, Satan has therefore no longer any
rights in us. But that is a merely negative fact.
There is a positive one also. God has not only
removed all that was in the way of his eternal
purpose by removing the old creation; he has
also secured all that is necessary to realize that
purpose by bringing in a new creation—his new
Man. "Christ being raised from the dead dieth no
more; death no more hath dominion over him"
(verse 9). The purpose revealed in Genesis 1 and
lost in Genesis 3 is not lost for good. What God
could not secure in the first man he obtained in
the second; and that second Man is on the
throne. No wonder the New Testament writer

dares to reapply the psalmist's words: "What is man, that thou art mindful of him? Or the son of man, that thou visitest him? Thou crownest him with glory and honor." Thus he quotes the psalm, and then he exclaims: "We behold him ... even Jesus ... crowned!" (Psalm 8:4-6; Heb. 2:6-9). If the creation of mankind was intended to meet the need of God, that need has now at last been met. God has got his Man.

Genesis 1, Psalm 8 and Hebrews 2 are thus uniquely linked. Psalm 8 is of course poetry and sings of God's plan for mankind, but the significant thing is that in spite of the Fall the singer does not deviate. He only reaffirms the original plan of Genesis 1: "Thou madest him to have dominion." It has not changed. Moreover, he not only begins but ends his chant with the exclamation of praise: "How excellent is thy name in all the earth!"

The enemy has done his worst; man has been trapped into blaspheming God, and if you or I had composed this Psalm we would surely have followed the eighth verse with a cry of distress: "But alas, man has fallen; all is lost!" Not so the psalmist. It is as though he had forgotten the Fall completely, for he does not even allude to it. He leaps in thought across the whole history of redemption, and cries again, "How excellent!" Adam and Eve could fall, but they could not alter God's purpose that man should eventually overthrow Satan's power. His purpose stands unaltered and this excellence is to be known—where? In all the earth.

Nor is it in the Son of man merely that this

purpose is realized, but in the sons of men—
those "many sons" whom God is bringing to
glory. The psalmist is at pains to underline this
fact. Though the enemy do his worst, the rights
he has gained through the Fall have not proved
inalienable. Still among men there are those he
cannot touch. "Out of the mouths of babes and
sucklings hast thou established strength, because of thine adversaries, that thou mightest
still the enemy and the avenger" (verse 2). God
does not depend on great military leaders. Little
children, yea, very babes, are sufficient to quell
the hosts of his foes.

As we saw, Hebrews 2 draws its inspiration
from this Psalm. Yet it goes a step further. While
reaffirming God's purpose in creation and the
goal to which it points, it does more than this.
Looking back realistically over the course of
fallen man's dark history it establishes now that
God's purpose in redemption and recovery is di-
rected to the identical end. In all the new circumstances that redemption has called into being, the plan is still unchanged. God has not
abandoned his goal. Moreover, from the writer's
viewpoint beyond the triumph of the Cross he
can confidently reaffirm the psalmist's affirma-
tion of faith. So, far from all being lost, it is true
to say that in Christ the end *has been* secured.

Oh, yes, it is still the same plan: "He left nothing that is not subject to him" (verse 8). Appear-
ances would tend to deny this, so that "we see
not yet all things subjected to him." Yet true as
this is, the writer disregards it and at once pro-
ceeds triumphantly: "But we behold him who

hath been made a little lower than the angels,
even Jesus, because of the suffering of death,
crowned with glory and honor, that by the grace
of God he should taste death for every man"
(verse 9). And then, almost defiantly he adds:
"that he might bring to nought ... the devil"
(verse 14).

What man was to do on earth for God, and
failed to do, our Lord Jesus has accomplished.
He "tasted death for everything" (as the original
Greek implies—not just "for every man"). That is
to say, it was not for man's redemption alone that
he died but for that of the whole creation, and,
going back further, for the recovery of the Father's purpose in the complete oversetting of the
Satanic world order.

Thus it comes about that today the Church has
a definite responsibility before God to register
the victory of Christ in the devil's territory. If
there is to be a testimony to the principalities
and powers, if the impact of Christ's sovereignty
through his Cross is to be registered in the spiritual realm, it can only be as the judicial foothold
in our hearts of the "pretender" in the race is met
and, by the same Cross, removed and repudiated.
For God's object is still that man should "have
dominion." Our work for him does not stop with
proclaiming a Gospel that was designed merely
to undo the effect of Genesis 3, marvelous as was
that undoing. God wants also to take us back
further to Genesis 1 itself. He wants us in Christ
to regain the moral dominion over his foe that
was there in view, and thus effectively to restore
the earth to him. This is surely why, as Paul tells

us, "the earnest expectation of the creation waiteth for the revealing of the sons of God" (Romans 8:19).

The Gospel of salvation is necessary and vital in order to meet man's need. But if as God's servants we are only laboring for others we are missing God's first aim in creation, which was to supply not merely man's need but his own. For as we have said already, the creation of man was to meet the need of God. Thus if today we are going to meet God's need we must go a step further and deal with Satan himself. We must steal back from him his power, evict him from his territory, spoil him of his goods and set free his captives—for God. The question is not merely, Of what account are we in the winning of souls? Rather is it, Of what account are we in the realm of principalities and powers? And for that there is a price to pay.

It is often possible to move men when it is quite impossible to move Satan. The plain fact is that it costs much more to deal with Satan than to win souls. It demands an utterness of spirit Godward that in itself effectually deprives Satan of any moral ground in us he may claim to possess. This is the costly thing. God in his merciful love for the lost can often bypass and overlook in his servants what one might justly feel to be appalling weakness and even failure. But while he may do this for the soulwinner, when it comes to our dealing with the devil it is another matter.

Evil spirits can see right through the witness of man. They can tell when it is compromised by being halfhearted or insincere. They are aware

when we are holding back a part of the price.
Looking at us they are under no illusions as to
whom they can safely defy or ignore; and con-
versely, they know perfectly well against whom
they are powerless. "Jesus I know, and Paul I
know; but who are ye?" (Acts 19:15). Because
they believe, they know when to tremble. And
let me say this: since our most important task is
their overthrow, it is better always that we
should have the witness of evil powers than the
praise of men.

But the price of this witness to the principalities and power is, I repeat, an utterness of
allegiance to God that is unqualified. To enter-
tain our own opinions or desires, or to prefer our
own variant and contrary choices, is simply to
present the enemy with his advantage. It is, in
short, to throw the game away. In any other
sphere there may perhaps—I do not know—be
room among our motives for something of self-
interest, without appreciable loss. But never, and
I repeat never, in this. Without such utterness for
God nothing can be achieved, for without it we
make even God powerless against his enemy.

So I say it once again: the demand is very high.
Are you and I here on earth, utterly committed,
utterly given to God himself? And because this is
so, are we tasting even now the powers of that
future glorious age? Are we reclaiming territory
from the prince of this world for the One whose
alone it rightly is?

11
Robbing the Usurper

"Christ Jesus came into the world to save sinners." Since in the eternal purpose of God it is man (and not some other being) who is to have dominion, it is natural and right that our compassion should be drawn out to those sinners. Notwithstanding anything said hitherto, we might well feel that in this brief day of grace the winning of souls to the Savior of the world is perhaps the supreme means available to us of robbing Satan of his spoils. Certainly were "man" himself our theme, we should give a big place at this point to the subject of soul-winning.

But we have dealt with evangelism already elsewhere.[1] Instead, therefore, I propose in closing these studies of "the world" to take another and more materialistic area of Satan's dominion by way of practical illustrations of the art of "despoiling the strong man." I refer to the field of finance.

Money is opposed to God. The Word of God speaks of it as the mammon of unrighteousness (Luke 16:9). Since Jesus says, "Make to yourselves friends by means of the mammon of unrighteousness," he clearly cannot mean to describe it as the mammon that you have obtained through unrighteous dealings. He is therefore saying that the mammon itself is unrighteous. What is being brought before us here is not the unrighteous means by which money is procured, nor the unrighteous use to which money is put, but *the unrighteous character of money*. Money in its essential character is evil. We talk of "clean money" and "dirty money," but in God's sight there is only dirty money. The man who knows God knows the character of money. He knows that money in itself is evil.

If you would test the character of anything, you only need to enquire whether that thing leads you to God or away from God. Money invariably leads away from God. Jesus lays down clearly in verse 13 the principle that it is impossible to serve God and mammon, though I think that even without his statement, most of us would be convinced that this is so. For experi-

[1] *What Shall This Man Do?* London, 1961, Chapter 3.

ence tells us that God and mammon are never on the same side; mammon is always set over against God.

Of course it would be possible to interpret Jesus' words more widely, and to see "mammon" as representing everything in general that opposes itself to God. But the apostle Paul helps us to pinpoint money as the means the world uses most successfully to draw us away from God. "They that desire to be rich," he says, "fall into a temptation and a snare and many foolish and hurtful lusts, such as drown men in destruction and perdition. For the love of money is the roots of all kinds of evil: which some reaching after have been led astray from the faith, and have pierced themselves through with many sorrows" (1 Tim. 6:9, 10). In other words, if anything can lead us astray from God, money will.

The essence of the world is money. Whenever you touch money you touch the world. The question arises, How can we take a thing which we know assuredly to be of the world, and yet not become involved with the world system? How can we handle and do business with money, that most worldly of worldly things, and not, in doing so, become implicated with Satan? Still more to the point, since nothing can be done today without paying for it, how is it possible for us to take money, that thing which is a supreme factor in building up the kingdom of antichrist, and use it to build up the kingdom of Christ?

The widow who dropped her mite into the temple treasury did something so acceptable to the Lord that she received from him special commendation. What in fact she did was just this: she took something out of the kingdom of Satan and contributed it to the kingdom of God. And Jesus approved. So how, let us ask ourselves, is such a transfer made? How is it possible to take money, which in its character is essentially unrighteous, and with it build up the kingdom of God? How can you make sure that all connection between the world and the money in your pocket has been severed? Do you dare to say that none of the money in your possession figures in Satan's books?

On every Roman *denarius* there was an image of Caesar. In Jesus' words, all such coins "are Caesar's." How could the connection between Caesar and that coin be severed? Money is a thing of the world. It is an essential part of the world system. How then can it be taken out of the world that claims it and devoted to God for his use?

In Old Testament times a rigid principle was laid down. "No devoted thing, that a man shall devote unto the Lord of all that he hath, whether of man or beast, or of the field of his possession, shall be sold or redeemed: every devoted thing is most holy unto the Lord" (Lev. 27:28). In other words, there is no true devotion without destruction. If in those days a sheep was devoted to God, it was not placed before him to remain there a living sheep and to bring forth lambs; it was placed before him to be sacrificed. "It shall certainly be put to death" (verse 29). Its destruction was the sign of its acceptance.

All money that is truly devoted to God must

come under the principle of destruction; that is to say, it must cease to exist as far as the world is concerned, and it must cease to exist also as far as I am concerned. When our Lord commended the widow for putting her two coins into the treasury, he observed that she had put in her *bios,* that is, her life. "She of her want did cast in all that she had, even all her living" (Mark 12:44). Many people just put money into the treasury of the Lord; she put her life in with her money. In other words, when that money went out of her possession, her life went out with it. In giving her two coins she gave her all.

If your money is to come out of the world, then your life will have to come out of the world. You cannot keep your self back and contribute anything significant to God. You cannot *send* your money out of the world at all: you can only *bring* it out of the world!

Thus it is no easy matter to transfer money from the realm of Satan to the realm of God; it involves travail. To convert souls from Satan to God is in fact easier than to convert money from Satan to God. By the grace of God men and women may be won to him whether or not we ourselves are devoted in any utter sense; but this is not so with money. It takes great spiritual power to convert our shekels, which in their character are evil, into shekels of the sanctuary. Money needs converting as truly as men need converting; and the money can, I believe, be made anew (if in a rather different sense) as truly as souls can be made anew. But your bringing of an offering of money to the treasury will not in

itself change the character of the money you offer. Unless your life goes out with your money it
cannot be released from the kingdom of Satan
and transferred to the kingdom of God. The spiritual value of your work for God will largely depend on whether or not the money you handle
has been delivered from the world system. I ask
you, Has it? Can you claim that there is no
money in your hand that belongs to the world?
Are you able to say now that your money is no
longer a part of the *kosmos,* for it has all been
converted? Are you willing to tell God: "I will
convert all the money I earn by labor, and all the
money I receive by gifts, that it all may be
thine?"

To Paul the principle was very plain: We want
you, not yours. Of the Macedonian saints, who
out of their poverty contributed so liberally, he
said that "first they gave their own selves to the
Lord," then they gave their money (2 Cor. 8:5).
Paul had his training in the Old Testament,
where the consecration of material gifts was always connected with the consecration of those
who brought the gifts. His reasoning may have
had its roots there.

For it may sound startling, but it is true, that
God has a limited supply of money, whereas Satan's supply is unlimited. You wonder perhaps
how this statement can be reconciled with that
other one, that all the silver and the gold are his.
Yet our Lord Jesus himself says that there is that
which belongs to God and that which belongs to
Caesar. Ultimately no doubt all material things
belong to God as Creator, but the amount of

money in God's treasury today is limited by the number of people who are devoted to him.

If I had lived in Old Testament times I could have calculated immediately the amount of money in the sanctuary. I should have inquired the total number of the children of Israel and reckoned half a shekel of silver for the redemption of each of them (Exod. 30:11-16). To that I should have added five shekels per head for the redemption of each of the firstborn of Israel in excess of the Levites (Num. 3:39-51). And then to these two amounts I should have added the valuation, according to the shekel of the sanctuary, put upon each individual who of his free will devoted himself to the Lord (Lev. 27:1-8). Yes, it is the number of God's people that determine the amount of God's money. The margin of wealth in God's treasury is based on the number of people devoted to him.

Here, then, is a vital question for each one of us to answer: Does the money I am touching today represent shekels of the sanctuary or the mammon of unrighteousness? Whenever I receive a dollar, or whenever I earn a dollar, let me make sure that that dollar is instantly converted from world currency into the currency of the sanctuary. Money can be our destruction, but money can also be our protection. Do not despise money; its value is too real for that. It can be of great account to the Lord. If you yourself come heart and soul out of the world, then you can, if God so wills it, bring many precious things out of the world with you. When the Israelites came out of Egypt they brought away much treasure

with them. They spoiled the Egyptians, and the
spoil they carried away with them went to construct the Tabernacle. Some too, we recall, went
to construct a golden calf and was lost to God.
But when God's people left Egypt the Tabernacle, at least in its materials, left Egypt with them.
Egyptian gold, silver, copper, linen—all was
converted and contributed to the sanctuary of
God.

If you can find that reality in Old Testament
times, how much higher still must be the standard set in the New! The New Testament key to
all finance is that we hold nothing to ourselves.
"Give, and it shall be given unto you," those
were our Lord's words (Luke 6:38) and not,
"Save and ye shall grow rich"! That is to say, the
principle of divine increase is giving, not stor-
age. God requires of every one of us propor-
tionate and not just random giving. He desires,
that is to say, giving that is not subject merely to
the whim of the moment but that is the fruit of a
definite covenant reached with him about the
matter—and stuck to.

This is because the real secret of spoiling
Satan is, as we saw, personal dedication. For us
to be redeemed from the world and not as a consequence offer ourselves to God is an utterly impossible thing. "Ye are not your own; for ye were
bought with a price" (1 Cor. 6:19, 20). It matters
not whether we follow a profession or trade that
brings us an income from the world, or occupy
ourselves solely in preaching the Word and depend for our sustenance upon the gifts of God's
people, there is only one road before us, not two.

We are all equally dedicated to God and we are all his witnesses. It is simply not true that preaching the Gospel in itself is clean and business unclean, so that those who engage in the latter must become so tainted as to be of less account to God. What matters is simply that God, and not our business, must be the center of our lives.

"Love not the world, neither the things that are in the world." You have an anointing from the Holy One: live by it! Give yourself to God; live for him wholly and utterly; see to it that, where you personally are concerned, the things of this world are scored off Satan's books and transferred to God's account. For "the world passeth away, and the lust thereof: but he that doeth the will of God abideth for ever."